Praise for

DESIGNED FOR MORE

"As long as followers of Christ stay in their comfortable silos and tribes, the world will never experience the full power of the Church. *Designed for More* gives us a beautifully memorable and practical way forward to become the united body of Christ. Don't miss this book."

—Mark Batterson, *New York Times* bestselling author of *The Circle Maker* and lead pastor of National Community Church

"It is time we come alive to see that disunity in Christ robs the Church of its collective power. The change-makers of the future will be those who bring people together, and *Designed for More* gives us exactly the vision . . . to become the unifying leaders our world needs. Thank you, Lucas and Mike, for diving into this much-needed conversation."

—Tyler Reagin, president of Catalyst and author of *Life-Giving Leader*

"A lot of us talk about the importance of unity, but few of us are given a practical guidebook of how to work towards unity. Lucas and Mike help expand the view of our flock, with the urgency unity requires. This message is not about compromising; this is about working past our fragmented and fractured 'playgrounds' for the unity God demands and desires for each of us."

—Esther Fleece, speaker and author of *No More Faking Fine*

"*Designed for More* brilliantly draws applicational truths from a rare phenomenon in the sky to everyday life in community."

—David Nasser, author, pastor and senior vice president of Liberty University

"The world is waiting for the church to come together and be the interconnected movement that best offers God's love and grace to all. *Designed for More* offers you and I what we need: a compelling vision for why unity matters and practical steps for us to move forward."

—Kara Powell, PhD, executive director of the
Fuller Youth Institute and co-author of *Growing Young*

"Few books inspire me to a second read. Not so with *Designed for More*. What a book! Lucas and Mike frame a picture of the beauty and power of the Kingdom: thousands of starlings in a sky ballet. Through biblical exegesis, science, and years of experience, they chart a path to wholeness and redemptive power. I love it. Quite simply, it makes me want to grab the hands of a band of friends and say, 'Let's fly!'"

—Dick and Ruth Foth, authors of *Known:
Finding Deep Friendships in a Shallow World*

"This is no time for soft and isolated Kingdom work. These are post-Christian times, and none of us is as good as more of us—in unity. *Designed for More* will awaken you again to Jesus' call to unity and give you the lens we all need for intentionally shaping collaborative Kingdom initiatives."

—Dr. Larry Acosta, founder and CEO of
Urban Youth Workers Institute

"The spaces that separate people, communities, and cultures exist because of the historical patterns that shape our approach to one another. My friends Lucas and Mike guide us in expanding our mindsets into singular formations that eliminate the warfare of separation."

—Fred Oduyoye, founder of Reachable Reconciliation

"To take a phrase from the latter part of *Designed for More*, this book is fused with 'radical optimism.' But don't mistake radical optimism for sentimental idealism. These pages give us a frank account of the challenges we face in being the unified Body of Christ. But they also call us to practical, ministry-tested action steps that we can take as pastors, youth pastors, teachers, and followers of the Lord who prayed that we 'might be one as [He] and the Father are one.' What in the world would happen if we read this book and took seriously its splendid, big-dream invitation?"

—Duffy Robbins, author and
professor of Christian Ministry at
Grove City College, Grove City, PA

"After reading *Designed for More*, I feel more empowered than ever to implement change in the name of our Lord Jesus Christ. Using the starlings and their murmuration, God shows us, through His creation, how to do His work by unifying individuals into a cohesive and effective unit. *Designed for More* not only identifies our underachieving of God's goals but clearly lays out a game plan for each of us to get back on track. Great book, and let's get started!"

—Rich Seban, former CEO of Hostess

"I loved this book! Every chapter brought inspiration and hope. It caused me to crave the deeper unity that only Christ can give."

—Jim Burns, PhD, president of HomeWord and
author of *Understanding Your Teenager* and
The Purity Code

"Real change will come when we take the first step in changing the way we think. Lucas Ramirez and Mike DeVito provide a fresh look at an old problem...the lack of unity among the Christian church. They do this by confronting head on the thinking that pulls the church apart and then provide clear pathways to drawing us back together for the sake of God's kingdom."

—Brian L. Cress, director of Denomination and
Youth Mobilization for International Justice Mission

"In these hurried days of the *too's*—too little time, too little joy, and too little love from my foes, friends, and self—*Designed for More* brought me back towards my God-granted peace and purpose."

—Ron Kitchens, senior partner at
Southwest Michigan First

"Lucas writes like he speaks—with flair, passion, inspiration, and insight. In *Designed for More,* Lucas and Mike fuel our desire for biblical unity. They expand our vision of how our spiritual gifts thrive in the context of 'one body.' The truths come down to earth with their practical applications and clarifying principles. Through the beautiful metaphor of how God unites starlings in flight, you find yourself dreaming of the revolutionary impact. If only the body of Christ followed suit!"

—Paul Fleischmann, president emeritus of
National Network of Youth Ministries and
founder of Better Together Resources

"I am an enthusiastic collaborator. Advocating for unity is the song I want to sing as a member of the choir. So I was honestly surprised at how much this book moved me; I didn't think I had to be moved! *Murmuration* is a brilliant metaphor for how God's people can practice tactical routines of faithfulness that result in unity. Jesus Christ, the Word of Creation, reveals His awe-inspiring design skills in the beautiful movements of starlings. Now may Jesus, the Head of His Church, choreograph our dance together for His resounding glory in the world!"

—Dr. Dave Rahn, senior ministry advisor for
Youth for Christ USA

DESIGNED FOR MORE

*Unleashing Christ's Vision for
Unity in a Deeply Divided World*

LUCAS RAMIREZ
with Mike DeVito

NASHVILLE NEW YORK

FaithWords
Hachette Book Group
1290 Avenue of the Americas, New York, NY 10104
faithwords.com
twitter.com/faithwords

First Edition: June 2018

FaithWords is a division of Hachette Book Group, Inc. The FaithWords name and logo are trademarks of Hachette Book Group, Inc.

The publisher is not responsible for websites (or their content) that are not owned by the publisher.

The Hachette Speakers Bureau provides a wide range of authors for speaking events. To find out more, go to www.hachettespeakersbureau.com or call (866) 376-6591.

The author is represented by Alive Literary Agency, 7680 Goddard Street, Suite 200, Colorado Springs, Colorado, 80920, www.Aliveliterary.com

Library of Congress Cataloging-in-Publication Data has been applied for.

ISBNs: 978-1-5460-3298-4 (hardcover), 978-1-5460-3296-0 (ebook)

Printed in the United States of America

LSC-C

10 9 8 7 6 5 4 3 2 1

Lucas Ramirez Dedication:

To Thea. The love of my life and fiercest cheerleader.

Llenas mi vida con canción

Arrulado en tu amor

Solo sabe Dios cuanto te amo

Mike DeVito Dedication:

To my parents, Joe and Mary, and to my wife, Kristi,
who all have continually encouraged my passion for unity.

Contents

Part Three
PRACTICAL STEPS TO HELP SPARK A
MURMURATION MOVEMENT

Introduction

Origins

Unity. Unfortunately, this word has grown tired, exhausted understandably by our failed attempts to embrace it. As a result, unity no longer presents itself as the most exciting or innovative answer to the problems facing our Church and world.

Even the word itself, "unity," evokes negative reactions in some Bible-believing Christians. Yet, despite our perceived fatigue with the term, we need to hear again the call in Hebrews 3:15 to not harden our hearts. Now is the time to allow the Spirit to guide us in all truth to see that *unity is the catalyst for unleashing the mission of the Church in the world today.*

Unity is when all followers of Jesus realize their interconnectedness and pursue the oneness as seen in the Triune God in order to become one with God and with each other—for His glory and the expansion of His kingdom. This biblical vision is a dynamic process that is not intended to be merely an add-on or a special interest of a few. This is also not an organizational or institutional merger. It requires an internal change that manifests through external action. Like a puzzle being completed, we bring our gifts and strengths to the table for the bursting forth of our unified mission.

Unity is arguably the gateway to the very mission of the Church. The vocational calling of Jesus' followers is to love sacrificially, spread the good news of His atoning sacrifice on the cross, and partner with God in the renewal of all things. To accomplish this calling, unity must be the common component that permeates our movement if we have any chance at success.

If you are not nodding your head in agreement yet, then we dare you to read this book. If you've already bought into the idea, then this book will only catapult you further.

The truth is that if we want to care for the poor, welcome strangers, seek justice, clothe the naked, and preach the Gospel most effectively, we need unity. Unity must encompass all the efforts of the Church, regardless of where our specific passion or calling lies. Without it, we employ only low-leverage solutions.

If the Church is the main vehicle for growing God's kingdom, how can we be effective if we are divided? Despite our unimaginable potential as followers of Christ, we are held back because our house is defensive, judgmental, wounded, and siloed. **It is time for us to be the answer to Jesus' prayer in John 17 and catch the world's attention with jaw-dropping unity:**

> My prayer is not for them alone. I pray also for those who will believe in me through their message, that all of them may be one, Father, just as you are in me and I am in you. May they also be in us so that the world may believe that you have sent me. I have given them the glory that you gave me, that they may be one as we are one—I in them

and you in me—so that they may be brought to complete
unity. Then the world will know that you sent me and
have loved them even as you have loved me.

John 17:20–23 NIV

Each and every step we take toward unity delights the Lord,
no matter how big or small those steps may be. No matter if it
is true unity or collaboration (sometimes we collaborate and
think it's unity—more on this later), moving toward Him and
His vision is the only thing that matters, because for Jesus,
He saw with extreme clarity that the world will see His glory
and love through the *unity* of His followers. Though individual experiences may differ, churches and ministries that have
taken such a step have discovered this truth: *when believers,
churches, and ministries lay hold of their interconnectedness within
the body of Christ, their ministries and impact become boundless.*

Sadly, because of our busy schedules, egos, and past hurts,
far too few within the Body of Christ are presently engaged in
pursuing the fulfillment of Jesus' call for unity. We don't even
talk about it. We rarely teach on it.

The fact is, on all sorts of levels (not just race), Martin
Luther King Jr. was right: Sunday mornings are still the most
segregated time in the life of the Church. We have a serious
problem. The prophet Haggai records the Lord lamenting how
each of us hurries off to our own houses, leaving His house
in ruins: "You expected much, but see, it turned out to be
little. What you brought home, I blew away. Why?" declares
the LORD Almighty. "Because of My house, which remains a
ruin, while each of you is busy with your own house" (Haggai
1:9 NIV).

Are we so busy working on our local congregations or ministries—keeping our own house in order—that we have lost sight of the larger body? Are we too comfortable in our silos?

Designed for More answers these questions. This book is not a prescription for a new model of ministry. Rather, it is an invitation for the Body of Christ to discover God's great passion for unity and see the bigger picture so that we can finally operate within our true design. This is a call to action for unleashing the full potential of the Church through our unity. And this vision is not just for pastors or ministry leaders—we *all* have a role to play. We are speaking to you, believers who are ready to be culture-shifting trendsetters and show the world the reconciling power of the Gospel. We are speaking to you, Christ's followers who are tired of the division and know there is a better way. Together, we can spark a movement of massive proportions. Why? Because it is Christ's vision, not ours. And we want to be about Christ's business!

God designed His fellowship of believers for so much more power, finesse, efficiency, and beauty, but we have been held back by our current state of division. To grow into our true design, we need to know both the biblical imperative for being one body *and* we need practical steps forward. Mike and I hope to offer both of those in the following pages.

But unity itself is not the only goal. It's a tool—the vehicle and bridge to something greater. The ultimate goal is what a unified church produces. When believers make unity a priority and accept the invitation into the divine fellowship where perfect unity exists, we will begin to murmurate as one body. And the world will see what Jesus prayed for: His kingdom come here and now.

Part One

GOD'S GREAT PASSION FOR UNITY

This section will begin by revealing the story of how the Murmuration phenomena came alive for me (Lucas). After we explore our current fragmented, divided state as the Body of Christ, we will establish God's great design for unity by looking at Scripture and nature. The juxtaposition of our current reality and Jesus' vision will hopefully give us a framework for what we might be missing as followers of Christ. This will generate the creative tension and urgency we need to raise the importance of unity in the Church. Let's go!

Chapter 1

The Murmuration

For since the creation of the world God's invisible qualities—his eternal power and divine nature—have been clearly seen, being understood from what has been made, so that people are without excuse.

—Romans 1:20 NIV

It snuck up on me. A moment of awe and wonder that I had not expected at 4:30 a.m. This particular morning, I rose early to pray, research, and write (with small children in the house, you have to fight for those moments). As I sat down at my computer, I stumbled upon a video that took me by surprise. What came to life on my screen was a *Murmuration*: a flock of starlings, numbering in the thousands, creating moving art in the sky. The aerial ballet was mesmerizing. Hypnotic, and unlike any other bird formation I had ever seen. Driven to awe, poets have described a Murmuration as *madness in the sky.*[1] I watched the birds fly together in sync, twisting and turning, like a cloud that has suddenly come to life, creating beautiful shapes that shifted and changed in the air.

A Murmuration is one of nature's most beautiful displays of unified and collective movement. Named for the sound created by thousands of wings flapping, Murmurations occur as a flock of starlings comes together in the evening to roost. These formations occur in the later fall and early winter months, and although they have been spotted in several places around the world, the greatest concentration occurs in the United Kingdom.

To watch a flock of just fifty birds flying in unison is amazing, but now imagine a Murmuration with thousands, even hundreds of thousands of birds.[2] In Rome, up to five million starlings have been known to descend upon the city in the wintertime, drawn by the warmth. (Still images don't even come close to doing it justice; if you have not yet seen this phenomenon in motion, treat yourself and visit our site DesignedFor MoreBook.com for Murmuration videos.)

In the afternoon, the starlings begin to gather in protected areas such as reed beds, woods, or even man-made structures that provide extra protection. Then, at dusk, with only a few moments of sunlight left, as if breaking forth from an organized huddle, they suddenly take to the sky en masse. This is no ordinary flock of birds in flight. The beautiful theatrical display has a transfixing effect—a gift from nature of incredible proportions.

As the starlings erupt into a Murmuration, they swoop, dive, contract, and then explode in unison with incredible rhythm, speed, efficiency, and finesse. Despite the rapid and close-quarter movements of the formations, they consistently avoid collisions. Like a liquid cloud, the birds play mid-air aerobatics and create epic sweeping motions as if they obeyed a single conductor. The synchronized maneuvers are simply spectacular.

Unforgettable.

A madness in the sky.

GOING DEEPER

Have you ever felt awe in this way? Maybe you stood at the edge of the Grand Canyon looking out at the depth and breadth in front of you, or at a mountain lip as the sun rose glittering on fresh powdery snow. Maybe you've felt the coarse black Hawaiian sand between your toes, or gazed at the stars and felt the massive, breathtaking scale of it all.

Inside each of us, God has carved out a place to be filled with His wonder. Creation   mountains, sunsets, oceans, birds—can fill this inner space with worship and wonder for one simple yet profound reason: creation is a signpost to the very nature of God. Whatever your experience with feeling wonder may be, those moments are meaningful because they speak of who God is, what God is like, and what God values. Like art tells us about the artist, the very rhythm, order, and design of creation speak of God's character.

Romans 1 reminds us that from the very beginning His eternal power and divine nature have been clearly seen in what is made. In creation, we see the divine nature turned physical. The unfathomable made visible. The infinite expressed in finite means. God has put a message into creation—His nature *in* nature.

This is the exact wonder, worship, and revelation that I experienced as I watched the Murmuration video that early morning. I had seen a similar video of Murmurations once before, but this was the first time I *saw* it. As I watched the birds soar together in perfect harmony, I awoke to the magnificent metaphor God had hung in the sky. In this vivid example of unity and collective movement, I marveled at the sheer beauty of His design—and caught a glimpse of how beautiful the Church could be if we moved as one body. In this moment, I saw the Lord's vision for His Church and the higher potential we were designed for.

However, my heart simultaneously broke.

The bitter reality is that most of the time, the Church is in a fragmented and disjointed state. We fight, hold grudges, undermine one another's ministries, or just remain indifferent. We use public platforms to slander one another and promote our own agendas. Instead of growing in influence and transformative power, the Church is losing (and in some places, has already lost) credibility in today's culture.

But it doesn't have to be that way. Imagine what we could accomplish as a truly united body—the sky is literally the limit.

The deeper I studied Murmurations, the truth in Romans 1 became increasingly more evident. It became clear that through this Murmuration phenomena, God wanted to show us more than a beautiful metaphor—so much more. The deeper I studied new research on the starlings, the more I began to see that by learning from the bird's flight patterns and *how* the starlings murmurate, we, too, can learn how to soar without colliding and fly as one with great brilliance. In these pages, this phenomenon will not only be our central metaphor, but also our road map and launching pad to becoming the *unified* Body of Christ!

WHY DO STARLINGS MURMURATE?

For years, scientists were limited by technology in their ability to study Murmurations. But by using today's advanced video and analytic computer technologies, they have been able to more closely study the starlings' motions. The findings have been profound.

The starlings roost together in large numbers for greater warmth during the colder months, but the main reasons they flare into a Murmuration is for *protection from a common enemy.* Like an army showing its power in numbers, the Murmuration is a defense mechanism, as the group's movements disorient and deter predators. It is easy for a falcon to pick off a single bird, but it is much more difficult for a predator to fly into a hoard of starlings. As the starlings live together without fighting for turf, they successfully protect against danger. They know that to survive, they must unite and stick together.

HOW DO THE STARLINGS MURMURATE?

There is much debate among scientists about the cognitive abilities of birds. At the onset, researchers began wondering about the possibility of some telepathic transference occurring in the starlings. Could it be that starlings carry a higher intelligence than other birds? Do birds even have intelligence at all? What is intelligence anyway?

What did become clear to scientists, however, was that Murmurations do not occur because of some invisible network of connectivity formed between the birds' brains. The phenomenon *emerges* when the birds follow a core set of behavioral rules. They have an ability to focus on and execute core behaviors that benefit the whole system. It is no coincidence that the individual members benefit in the end. The truth is that complex order does not necessarily come from complex behavior or thought—powerful implications that we'll unpack later.

The mechanics of extremely coordinated turn-pin movements are anchored in these core behavioral rules. This is critical. The entire enterprise hinges on it.

The birds' intense commitment to these core behaviors produces what scientists call "emergent behavior." In other words, the Murmuration is a phenomenon that comes alive and "emerges" only when the group comes together and follows their core behaviors. By following the group rules, something almost mystical occurs—in their unique unity, their fellowship becomes an unbelievable force unattainable by any individual on their own.

WHAT DOES A MURMURATION SAY ABOUT GOD?

Romans 1 tells us that creation is a standing billboard to God's eternal power and divine nature. Think about the weight of that. Everything you see, touch, feel, and taste says something about God. His divine nature is woven into your friend's smile, a puppy's silky coat, and the sweet taste of honey. Amazing.

So then, if the Murmuration phenomena is a reflection of

God's character, what does it reflect exactly? What design has the Creator saturated into these bird formations?

The answer is exquisite: the Murmuration is a flowing, swirling, swooping signpost that declares God's great passion for unity. The individual pieces become a new whole to accomplish a goal that would have otherwise been impossible. Consider the myriad places God has placed this truth throughout nature. There are so many colors and hues, materials of varying density and texture, that all come together to form a cohesive whole. In just one part of creation, we take for granted the many individual elements uniting to complete a perfect tableau: sky, water, trees, stars, mountains all coming together to form a breathtaking landscape.

This essential part of God's character is not only in creation, it is also echoed repeatedly in the Scriptures. In fact, Genesis 1 reveals that unity within diversity was infused into the very fabric of creation from the very beginning. The Godhead, the ultimate picture of unity within diversity, poured His essence into creation, like musicians pour their heart into their music. This rhythm is all around us. Even inside of us. When we hear reverbs and echoes of this voice calling for oneness, shalom, and completion, our desire is to join this irresistible ballet. Most of the time, however, like a child grasping a handful of sand, unity slips through our fingers.

BACK UP

But let's back up for a minute.

How did the flight pattern of Lucas, a thirty-something

South American living on the East Coast, connect with Mike, a ministry veteran North American from the West Coast? You guessed it: we met in the Philippines.

In early 2014, thousands of miles from our respective, comfortable, middle-class lives in the United States, caught in the crosshairs of a violent and historic typhoon, our flight patterns intersected. It was by divine appointment that we connected through our mutual friend Brian Cress. Brian is the director of denominational and student mobilization for the International Justice Mission, an organization that fights slavery, trafficking, and injustice internationally. Brian put together a small team of student leaders from across the country to see firsthand the work of IJM and strategize together how we could further the cause of justice. Each of us came from our own ministry contexts, individual experiences, and paradigms. But over the course of ten days, together we witnessed the heart-wrenching realities of human trafficking and slavery, and in the face of pure evil, our personal and unique differences within the group evaporated.

Brian exposed our group to IJM's work among those suffering from heinous injustices in the Philippines, because he recognized that when inspired and united, the Church is capable of moving mountains, even the most violent and sinister. We as a group of very different individuals from different backgrounds all united in seeking a mutual vision of how we could help IJM overcome these evils.

Our group spent loads of time traveling to different areas of the Philippines in our van. It was during those stomach-churning, dizzying rides, while sharing within group discussions, that Mike and I connected. There, in a rare moment of lucidity, we saw that God had woven the same theme of unity into every fiber of our lives. We wondered if He was now weaving that theme into our lives together—to become part of the revolution He prayed for in John 17!

Designed for More consists of marrying our experiences with ideas from various disciplines including science, history, psychology, theology, sociology, and organizational leadership. It brings together over forty years of combined ministry experience and study. Mike and I work toward unity within diversity through our day-to-day work, Mike as the Southwest regional coordinator for the National Network of Youth Ministries overseeing networks in five states. He also serves as the ministry outreach coordinator at Biola University in California. And I serve as the director of The Gathering Place, an innovative student mentoring and Christian leadership development organization that impacts thousands of students annually. We don't just talk and teach about unity, we labor toward a united Church body—this is a passion that saturates our lives!

THE UNIVERSAL STRUGGLE

The unity reflected in nature is not easy to attain in human endeavors. One of the greatest struggles for leaders of all types is how to generate collective behavior.[3] Defining a common vision can be difficult, but *sustaining* movement toward that common vision is even harder. Organizations eventually break down if they are

> One of the greatest struggles for leaders of all types is how to generate collective behavior.

unable to bring cohesion to their many diverse parts, despite individual brilliance and talent.[4]

This struggle grows exponentially in today's culture with the mass of information that is readily available through technology. The saturation of information makes collective movement more difficult because information promotes a higher sense of individual opinion through exposure to many different perspectives.

Man's greatest search in philosophy has also been the search for unity within diversity. As Ravi Zacharias points out, the very word "university" speaks to our search for unity within diversity, and on every American coin is written *E pluribus unum*, "out of many one."[5] Despite our best efforts for finding this unity in our governments, companies, schools, and communities, it continues to elude us. We struggle not because it is impossible to hold, but because we have not used the proper containers.

The Christian Church is no different. In Christ we have the answers our world craves, but the world does not come to us for answers because many times we look just as lost and scattered as those without the Light. From the early Church and those early believers choosing between Apollos or Paul, to the Reformation and the Great Schism, and now our thousands and thousands of denominations globally, our story has been one of splintering. History and headlines show that followers of Christ have always struggled to sustain unity that produces collective movement.

But now it is time for a new way.

Followers of Christ have always struggled to sustain unity that produces collective movement. Now is the time for a new way.

OUR HOPE

Despite our failed attempts at being the united body of Christ, we do have reason for great hope. **The same One who infused unity into creation still stands as the perfector and author of the story, a story where He gathers His bride into one collective whole for His purposes.** It is a story where He sums up all things in heaven and on earth under His banner. Although unity was broken at the fall of man when sin entered creation, the death and resurrection of Christ is the hinge upon which unity between God and creation was restored. The message of the cross is that the greatest of enemies are reconciled. Now, He invites us into a divine fellowship and community where unity *is* possible. Through learning lessons from nature and Scripture, God is calling us to a better way.

For the first time, we are applying the research on Murmurations to human endeavors in order to unleash unity in the Church today. Not next year. Not at the Second Coming. Christ's invitation is for *today*!

But it goes even deeper. Jesus' death and resurrection was not simply to reunite God and creation; it was also to secure unity between brothers and sisters. Between neighbors. If by faith we believe Christ is Lord, repent of our sins, and choose to live under His Lordship, we enjoy reconciliation with God *and* with our neighbor.

We quickly forget that in the final hours before suffering an excruciating death, unity was a major priority for our Lord: "That all of them may be one, Father, just as you are in me and I am in you. May they also be in us so that the world may believe that you have sent me" (John 17:21 NIV). He could have prayed about so many things in those final moments, but in Jesus' longest recorded prayer, He spent his time focused on the unity of His followers.

We must ask ourselves: Is unity a priority for us as it is a priority for Christ?

God calls His followers to be angled mirrors of His love and reflect Him to the world. Therefore, our unity is critical in our witness of the Lord we serve: "By this everyone will know that you are my disciples, if you love one another" (John 13:35 NIV). John Armstrong, author and professor at Wheaton College, put it this way: "The real indicator of the church's faithfulness is not successful evangelization; it is our oneness."[6] It is time for this vision to catch fire in the Church.

Imagine what would happen if believers stepped into this calling and united in Christ. Our unity would not simply be an unseen aspect of spirituality; we would see unparalleled work accomplished if the two billion people worldwide who claim to follow Christ began to communicate and share resources. The Church would become *the* hub of disruptive entrepreneurs and innovative problem solvers for the largest issues facing our world. Our fellowship would be marked by radically selfless servants worldwide. Imagine the dollars we could redirect away from any duplication this would reveal and reinvest into new projects. We would freely unlock our relationships and connections to help others with no hesitation for how it would benefit us personally in the end.

The impact would not just be felt in who we are, but also in what we do. As we murmurate, the unparalleled healing, forgiveness, and restoration among believers would catch the world's attention.

So, if creation and Scripture declare the importance of unity, what can we do practically to protect and propel the unity Christ desires for His Church? We invite you to come and see how the Church can, through the power of the Holy Spirit, murmurate as we move and dance to the rhythms of unity.

MIND THE GAP—CULTIVATING CREATIVE TENSION

Today, God is waiting for His followers to murmurate. However, we have a serious problem: we have largely neglected that which God cares most deeply about—the unity of His followers. How can Christ's followers all over the world catch this vision and become a murmurating body?

Perhaps we can start by looking at what MIT professor and systems thinking expert Peter Senge calls "creative tension," a concept based upon scientific fact that tension always seeks resolution. He argues that individuals and organizations must learn how to generate "creative tension" to actualize our goals and visions.[7] This tension is the energy that helps us move the needle from point A to point B. Generally, we try to avoid or escape tension; however, we should not run away from *creative tension*, because it propels us toward accomplishing our goals and visions.

How does one cultivate creative tension? We need two things: (1) a clear vision and understanding of **where we want to be** and (2) a clear and realistic picture of **where we are**. When individuals and organization envision both of these things simultaneously, they are inevitably propelled toward their goal with the same kind of energy as when a rubber band, stretched to its limits, is released.

We can only see the gap between our status quo and our vision when we clearly see each of these elements at the same time. **The gap makes us uncomfortable, but there is power in it.**[8]

Can you see it? If we learn to continually cultivate a perspective of where we are and where we want to be, allowing Christ to define our dreams and desires, our lives will be filled with such exponential purpose and power that nothing will contain us.

Most of the time, however, our lives are so hurried, and the issues, events, or programs in our lives and ministries so urgent, that we don't spend the necessary time to consider where we are really going. This is not easy work, and it takes time. It is like trying to look at your reflection in a pool of water. If the water is disturbed, hurried, and in constant motion, it is impossible to see a clear reflection. However, when we slow down and the water begins to settle, we can see our reflection more clearly.

Busyness and hurry also keep us from confronting our fear that we may never actually fulfill our dreams. We are afraid to confront how far we actually are from our passions and goals. With no time to evaluate our vision for the future or identify our present-day reality, we miss out on the powerful forces that *creative tension* could produce in our lives to actually get us to realizing our dreams.

Becoming a *murmurating* Church will require the work of creative tension, only possible through a clear look at today's reality and the biblical vision for the Church. As we wrestle with adjusting our vision to become like Christ and take a fearless accounting of where we currently are, we will be able to use the tension as a catalyst to move toward Jesus' prayer in John 17.

So that is exactly what we want to do with the next two chapters.

In chapter 2, we will drill deeper to discover where we are as the universal body of Christ today. From examining the reality of more than thirty thousand churches and denominations,[9] we'll encounter the truth of what presently exists and juxtapose it with what Jesus prayed for.

In chapter 3, we will focus on God's design as we explore where we are called to be. We will unpack the unity modeled perfectly for us in the Trinity and taught about in the New Testament.

The pages that follow are designed to spark conversations. This level of work cannot be done in one spot, but rather must continue in local contexts, evaluating and considering the spatial and cultural influences in our communities. Our great hope is that by looking at our reality and the vision together, we will be blessed with an inescapable tension that causes us to creatively seek resolution for the existing gulf between where we are and the divine design of a unified body.

BEING AND DOING

The Murmuration offers a beautiful and memorable road map of solutions to the universal struggle of leaders and organizations. Within this natural phenomenon, we found hidden the lessons for unleashing the power of collective movement. If followers of Christ can catch the biblical vision for unity and apply principles from the Murmuration, believers will unleash the mission of the Church like never before.

Birds first taught us to fly and now they will teach us to unify!

To get there, the path consists of being and doing, because unity is something that is held both in the heart and hands. It is a state of mind in each person that turns into action. The movement must then go beyond the individual and make changes at the systemic level. As Cardinal Hume said, these structural changes and metanoia might feel like a death at first, but would in reality be a resurrection.[10]

While there have been bursts of collaboration in the modern Christian Church, disunity is one of the greatest limiting factors to our mission today. Christians remain largely unaware of the biblical call for unity. As a result, the Church is not regarded as a united body. We have not taken seriously Christ's clarion call to unity—having allowed contemporary cultural mind-sets to infringe upon that call. **It's time we become united in the power of the Holy Spirit because unity is not merely a supplement or an add-on; it is the gateway to unleash the mission of the Church.** Through relationships and strategy, learning new disciplines, and with radically optimistic leadership, the multicolored and many-tongued church of the twenty-first century has the potential to spark an organic movement that moves us into God's design and into the fulfillment of Jesus' prayer for the Church.

The Lord God Almighty has not called us to uniformity, but He has called us to be united in Him. What if churches and ministries all across the world, like a starling Murmuration, reached the point of completing one another rather than competing against one another? Would our impact not be earth shaking?

It's time to dream big.

The starling Murmurations cause the world to stop and stare. To study it. To share videos about it. It's time for the Church to be equally as captivating. It's time for our unity to be so compelling that it causes the world to stop and stare and to get wrapped up in the beauty of who God is. Come and see *the* Church as it was designed to be, today, as a starling Murmuration, sweeping, dancing, and moving for the glory of God as one body, visible to all.

Designed for Bigger, Better Playgrounds

> The great sin of our era is not the immorality of society but the disunity of the church...The sin of disunity has caused more souls to be lost than all other sins.
>
> —Max Lucado, Promise Keepers
> Conference, 1996

I absolutely love my little girl. When Luciana was four years old, my wife and I took her on an afternoon outing at the pier on St. Simons Island. It was a sunny, coastal Georgia day, and we went to the village area—a popular spot with shops, walking paths, and, in the span of about two hundred yards, two playgrounds. One has all the big, new equipment and the other is tiny and not very exciting. We happened to park in front of the not-so-exciting playground—directly in our path to the bigger, better playground. Our goal was always to go to the more exciting one, but something happened along the way. When we passed the small one, Luci ran over and started to play. I was surprised to see she was enjoying the low-grade mulch and sub-par aluminum. *Man, if she likes this, she will love the big playground*, I thought.

So, in my fatherly wisdom, I said, "Okay, Luci, let's go. There is an even better playground right over there." I pointed to the perfectly exciting jungle of plastic, which was in clear view and just a short walk away—at least if you are six feet tall. For a vertically challenged four-year-old, she could not see farther than the few feet of low-grade mulch around her.

When I suggested moving on, I was met with a shocking temper tantrum. Our happy outing was unraveling. "I am trying to help you," I said, forgetting that using logic with a four-year-old is like trying to put the toothpaste back in the tube. Despite my reasoning, she continued to throw a major fit: "I want to stay in *this* playground!" she yelled.

FRAGMENTED

It is easy to get stuck in our comfortable playgrounds, isn't it? I wonder if this is what God sees when He looks at His followers. Through the Scriptures and nature, God has shown us the greater design that He imagined for the Church—that we would be *one* body, bringing our collective strengths to the table, loving and serving one another as we build His kingdom throughout the world. But somewhere along the way, we got stuck in our smaller playgrounds. Like four flat tires, have we become immovable, unwilling to dream?

What if there is a bigger, better reality just around the corner that God has invited us into?

Today, the current reality of the Church is a fragmented state. We have bought the lie that journeying from our playground to the bigger and better one is impossible. We are planted in our scattered kingdoms, thinking we are safe behind our fortified walls.

> What if there is a bigger, better reality just around the corner that God has invited us into?

Yet sadly, our divided state doesn't bother us that much.

Before we go any further, it is important to note that evaluating our current reality is not an exercise in casting blame or judgment, but rather, in love, a way to call our fellowship to a better way. His people are divided, and we have all contributed in some way. We must ask: What does He see when He looks at the Church today?

God's heart is grieved. Lack of forgiveness, bitterness, and envy abound in the personal lives of believers and at the corporate level of our churches. In both private and public forums, Christians slander one another. We are so busy building our own brands we have no time left to build community-wide collective movements that mobilize the whole Body of Christ. Trends of competition and individualism significantly undermine the effectiveness of our mission. We are miniature isolated flocks.

Yes, we might have numbers globally, but we have lost the defensive power of *unified* numbers, preferring isolation in more comfortable habitats—playgrounds—that meet our individual preferences or opinions. "Disunity is a scandal to the gospel and a stumbling block to faith,"[1] says Sarah Hinlicky Wilson. Despite the universal claim among believers that there is one Lord and one Church, all the practical evidence of how we operate says differently.

Our public disunity points to an even deeper fragmentation of how we see ourselves versus how we actually operate.
Christians generally agree unity is something God desires and
we should work toward. But in reality, very little is done to
accomplish it. We don't see unity as a major priority.

The reality is, we have a crisis of fragmentation. And we
are not heartbroken at the current divided state in the Church.
Some of us declare weekly that we believe in "one, holy, catholic, and apostolic church," but our actions rarely match our
declarations about a universal Church. We either don't fully
know the biblical vision, or we see unity as unattainable and
consequently, we try not to think about it.

Church history, headlines, personal experience, and the statistics make us numb. Statistics show that 90 percent of African
Americans attend predominantly black churches[2] and at least
95 percent of white Americans attend mostly white churches.
In a survey done by Smith and Emerson of over twenty-five
hundred Americans, the majority cited division in the Church
as a major issue, specifically racial division.[3] Race is just one
marker—the enemy's strategy of division is working and our
fault lines run much deeper than race.

God's great story of reconciliation has been crippled because
the messengers of that story are unreconciled.

How can we expect the world to believe in the reconciliation power of the cross if
the Church is not living it?
The cross is the place where
the irreconcilable becomes reconciled,[4] but not just between
man and God, between men

> God's great story of
> reconciliation has been crippled
> because the messengers of
> that story are unreconciled.

too. In Christ, the spiritual sibling bond, and our relationship to those around us, is second only to our love for God—but we don't act that way. Churches split and take each other to court over property. Pastors scheme to steal the sheep of other pastors.

A pastor friend of mine recently told me a story about being at a conference for his denomination with many other pastors. He found a seat in the audience near some of the pastors from his region. During the service, a pastor from a local church in his community leaned up and whispered in his ear, "You know the Smith family that goes to your church? Yeah, they'll be coming to my church pretty soon." Envisioning myself in his shoes, admittedly my initial response might have been, "I oughta slap you." I'll actually leave all the slapping to the Holy Spirit. Unfortunately, this sort of thinking is commonplace and a symptom caused by an unholy desire for power, competition, profit, and fame.

MIKE'S STORY

A few years ago, I was meeting with a youth ministry leader in our city. They had a large impact and were doing significant ministry in the area. My desire was to invite him to be a part of our local network of leaders because we needed their strength in ministry. I told him that our focus was on connecting through relationships, the sharing of resources to develop strategies for reaching more teenagers with the Gospel. His response was quick and robust: "Oh, I don't have time." A bit shocked by his total lack of interest, I asked if he would be willing to at least pray with us. Again, his response was, "We pray together with my ministry team and don't have the time to pray with you." Everything within me screamed, "You're wrong!" I was angry that someone could be so arrogant that they felt they didn't need another part of the Body of Christ.

You have your story, too, I'm sure. Or at least you've heard one. There are church splits at the structural level and gossip at the interpersonal level. The list goes on—sin has divided us in both private and public forums. The majority of the Christian Church today is divided into groups that are homogeneous in color, thinking, preferences, political affiliation, social views, and theology.[5] And in a peculiar way, we are okay with this as long as we sense that our divisions are not charged by prejudice or hatred. It is estimated that there are over thirteen hundred denominations in the United States and over thirty thousand denominations worldwide.[6] That is about the same number of individual McDonald's restaurants that exist in the world.

Think about that.

We have as many denominations as there are McDonald's in the world.

What we thought were comfortable playgrounds and structures are really cages we have built around ourselves, keeping us from how we were designed to operate.[7] In the process, we lose out on the valuable contributions other perspectives bring to the table. This is why diverse teams outplay homogeneous teams every day of the week. Did you know that companies with diverse leadership generate better results and outperform their competition? It is not about the individual, but rather what the individuals can become when they unite and bring their strengths to the table. Not only is our most effective work done in unity, but it is also where the experience of doing the work is most satisfying and beautiful.

THERE IS REASON TO HOPE

The current reality is not *all* bleak—we are far from the *completion* that Christ wants for His Bride, but there are also powerful stories of believers beginning to *murmurate*.

A landmark, historic event happened just weeks before Mike and I met each other for the first time in the Philippines while there with the International Justice Mission in 2013.

Human trafficking is a major issue in the Philippines. To address this issue, for the first time in history the three main church councils there came together under one banner: to stop human trafficking.[8] The three councils sponsored a Freedom Forum on September 5, 2013—the Catholic Bishops' Conference of the Philippines (CBCP), the Philippine Council of Evangelical Churches (PCEC), and the National Council of Churches in the Philippines (NCCP). The issues facing their people are so urgent that they demanded unity. As Reverend Rex RB Reyes Jr. of the NCCP said: "We cannot do it by ourselves; we have to be together in this fight." The prayerful spirit of the forum rallied the delegates to continue the movement forward, and representatives of many churches and ministries signed a "Declaration of Solidarity Against Human

Trafficking." It was much more than just a one-day meeting—the bishops had follow-up meetings to put an actual strategy on paper and continue to build their relationships. They are serious about murmurating together to start a national movement that declares the love of Christ and sets the captives free.

Stories like these must give us hope and inspire us to move toward similar initiatives in our towns, cities, and places God has given us influence. In some areas, churches have come together to offer growing homeschool networks meeting space; in other cities, churches are beginning to murmurate to evangelize the lost or address growing juvenile detention trends. What are the issues in your backyard and how has God uniquely gifted your local churches to be the collective solution to those issues with a unified strategy? We cannot individually solve the problems in our communities, and the design was never for us to do so.

While there have been bursts of collaboration in the modern Christian Church, the state of the global Christian Church today is not of one visibly united body. A complex web of factors currently hinders the Murmuration of Christ followers. From disagreement on secondary doctrinal issues and tradition to personal preference or personalities, the web is large and frequently entraps us. Whatever the vehicle, the enemy's strategy is working. He knows that if he can keep us divided, we can never become a fully mature person or community of believers. The first step to correct our course is to identify our current state and shore up the areas of weakness and vulnerability.

We want to discuss just two of the main factors that we believe keep us in divided playgrounds: **ideas and culture**. We will explore how our own thinking and external cultural influences have landed us squarely in our smaller playgrounds.

IDEAS

Ideas are powerful. Think of the innovative products or revolutions sparked by ideas; for example, "We hold these *truths* to be self-evident, that all men are created equal, that they are endowed by their Creator with certain unalienable Rights, that among these are Life, Liberty and the pursuit of Happiness..." The American revolutionary war began because of "truths" and ideas that fueled action.

Our thought patterns, along with the ideas we have about ourselves and those around us, are very critical. These thought processes typically happen under the surface with little evaluation, but they have a great impact on how we act and subsequently impact the current divided state of the Church.[9] Understanding some of the psychological and sociological factors is critical to uncovering vulnerable places where our defenses are thin for protecting the unity in the Church. The thoughts below are not intended to be an exhaustive look at these fields, but just a few basics to get us going.

Ideas We Have About Ourselves

Part of the problem that we face is our egocentric perspective. We think of ourselves first, believing our perspective to be the best and most accurate. Jean Piaget, developmental psychologist, contributed much to this science in the early 1900s, influencing the work of Hastorf and Cantril in the mid-1950s. They published research on the egocentric tendencies in persons through an interesting study of people who all experienced the same football game.

In 1951, Princeton and Dartmouth were to play the last game of the season. Princeton's undefeated record contributed to the game's mounting suspense. The game resulted with a Princeton win, but was riddled with controversy over a broken leg, a broken nose, and the multitude of penalties on both sides. Everyone experienced the same football game from their individual perspective, forming their own diverse opinions. The Dartmouth fans were convinced the referees were cheating, and despite the win, the Princeton fans were convinced *they* were treated unfairly. From this, Hastorf and Cantril found that "Out of all the occurrences going on in the environment, a person selects those that have some significance for him from his own egocentric position in the total matrix."[10] We make ourselves the rule by which we measure the environment around us, and everything gets passed through that filter.

The psychologist Mark Leary states that humans are distinguished from animals because we have the ability to be the object of our own attention and actually think about ourselves in multifaceted ways.[11] Because of this unique ability, our natural tendency is to be the center of our own attention. We focus on ourselves. And although self-preservation and self-awareness are natural parts of creation, sin distorts this reality and produces selfishness and division.

Disunity eventually boils down to sin, but just saying it is "sin" doesn't really help. What sin specifically? What are the other elements influencing our sin? This egocentric current within us is important to identify because it becomes a major factor in keeping the Church in split reality. It is not just our logos that get in the way; it starts with our egos. Identifying these ideas in our own minds will help us find the answers.

People have a very difficult time recognizing their own egocentrism—this is basically a "dream within a dream" when we egocentrically think we are not egocentric.[12] Unchecked, this natural individualistic tendency produces immeasurable discord. Sometimes we cannot even know or see the full ramifications of our selfishness and self-centeredness. Cause and effect in human relationships is not always measurable immediately in time—that is why this is so dangerous. We may not even know we broke something, so we never have the chance to fix it.

There is a turning point, however. This ability to be the object of our own attention also possesses great power for good. Leary points out that being self-aware "permits a level of self-analysis and self-evaluation."[13] This ability God gave us can be a blessing or a curse. We can use this ability to promote pride, or we can use this ability to honestly look inward and identify areas for growth. It takes hours of self-reflection, however, to be able to see into our hearts clearly. Mostly, we are too controlled by the *urgent* all around us and the sin inside of us. Rather than using the "self" for good, we default to our natural sin state of egocentrism, ultimately contributing to the division of the Church.

Ideas We Hold About Others

My father-in-law recently shared with me an experience he had in his church while serving as an Anglican priest in the Washington, D.C., area. Their church rented meeting space in a business complex for their Sunday morning worship. Then, one day the vacant space directly next to theirs was rented out to another church. This quickly created some sound issues because the two churches shared a wall. The new church next door leaned on a contemporary music style for worship, and their band practice happened while my father-in-law's church was having their morning service.

You can imagine that the contemplative Anglican service with communion was not the same while drums, bass, and guitar were going full blast next door. Eventually, pastors of both churches met to work out the scheduling issues, and the situation seemed to be resolved.

Except it wasn't.

After one Sunday of quiet, the band resumed their normal practice time. Hearing the music again and knowing what a distraction it was for their service, my father-in-law made the quick decision to leave the service while his parishioners were greeting each other, run next door, and politely ask the band members to wait twenty minutes so that his service could finish.

I wish I could have been there to see him walking down the sidewalk of the strip mall in his white priestly robes to confront the musicians! I'm envisioning an Elijah move as he "gathered up his garments" (1 Kings 18 ESV). When he walked into the other church, interrupting the band practice, the music stopped, creating awkward silence as the band and my father-in-law just stared at each other. My father-in-law told them how the noise was bothering his worship service. The drummer, seemingly the leader of the group, responded with a chilling, "Well, you're bothering us too."

How do you like that for unity, common strategy, and working together in harmony?

Two churches, two separate representations of Jesus to the world, right next to each other, "bothering" each other. How can we ever change the world in this state?

One of the reasons churches end up bothering one another is because we develop group identities with people who are similar to us—our "in-group." Simultaneously we develop ideas (or perceptions) of what *others* are like—the "out-group." The danger zone occurs when groups develop a strong sense of identity and *only surround themselves with like-minded people*. These groups develop what social psychologist Christena Cleveland calls the *gold standard effect*: "Basically, the gold standard effect leads us to believe that not only are *we (in-group)* different from *them (out-group)*, but we are also better than them"[14] (emphasis and parentheses added). Cleveland believes that this is one of the main causes for divisions between groups. Logically it lines up. If my egocentric perspective is reinforced continually by my in-group of homogeneous and like-minded people, the explosive formula for judgment and rejection of others and disunity is all there.

Exclusive groups need bias. Borrowing a phrase from Reinhold Niebuhr, Smith and Emerson call this bias the "ethical paradox of group loyalty."[15] The basic idea is that even though a group, let's say for our purposes an individual local church, is made up of loving and self-sacrificing individuals, the in-group mentality actually *mutates* the individual unselfishness into group selfishness. In other words, group loyalty makes it very difficult for people to have empathy or understanding for those not in their clique. It is an effective protection mechanism for the group, but it delivers devastating outcomes for the Church.

All of this is rooted in our *ideas of others*. **The key to overcoming the gold standard effect is to expand our view of our flock.** Whether we view someone as part of our family or not will change the ideas we have about others. It is not easy to change our thought patterns, but if we expand our in-group to incorporate those in our out-group, we will fulfill what Paul calls us to in Ephesians:

> Always be humble and gentle. Be patient with each other, making allowance for each other's faults because of your love. Make every effort to keep yourselves united in the Spirit, binding yourselves together in peace. For there is one body and one spirit, just as you have been called to one glorious hope for the future. There is one Lord, one faith, one baptism, one God and Father of all, who is over all, in all, and living through all.
>
> Ephesians 4:2–6 NLT

To become the massive and beautiful flock we were designed to be, we must take captive the ideas we have about others.

CULTURE

When Jesus prayed for you and me, His prayer was not that we would be removed or sheltered from culture, but that we would be kept from the evil one in the midst of culture (John 17:15). My father, a professor at Eastern University, puts it this way: our goal in discipleship is not to remove people from the ocean of culture, but rather to teach them how to swim.

Isn't that our desire for our children? Not to be in a disconnected bubble, but that they may have the tools to stand strong in truth amid an ever-changing cultural landscape? This is what Christ wants for us too. He knew the culture, as a human construct, would push against unity. He knew that because of sin, the mainstream currents would drive us from our design. But He also knew that with His help, we could stand strong.

There has always been great tension between the Church and surrounding culture. And rightfully so. But sometimes it's hard to discern which impacts the other. When it comes to our current reality, we must identify that we have allowed the dominant cultural trait of *competition* to hold a prominent place in the Church—both in structure and thought.[16]

Dominant Trait: Competition

In our culture, competition is god. Many economists have argued that the more competition we have in an economy, the more beneficial it will be for the people.[17] When there is competition, the consumer benefits. For example, if there is only one shop in town to get your coffee fix, then you will gladly pay whatever price they set. But when a new coffee place opens in the same town, prices will inevitably drop and customer service will get better. With competition, you can choose where to sip your latte. As a result of competition, each coffee shop will get better to attract as many customers as they can.

Competition always makes things better!

Right?

An entrepreneurial spirit and competition in the marketplace are amazing things. However, is it wise to apply those mind-sets when we approach the Church?

The truth is, when applied to the fellowship of believers, competition reduces the Church to nothing more than a manufacturer of a product. But we, the Church, are called to greater works. And Jesus is not a product, He is a person. The Scriptures call us to be vehicles for His love through a spiritual family (where free market principles do not apply), and not a corporation. In Jesus' final prayers in John 17 He asks that the Church be one so that others will believe in Him. *In other words, the world is going to look at us and then decide what they believe about Jesus.* **So the question is, do we believe our call is to be better than the church next door or to help the church next door become better?**

I have been blessed to experience ministry in many different settings. During my years of volunteering or interning at ministries, I never once concerned myself with the numbers or size of the ministry. As an intern or a volunteer, for me ministry was all about relationships and impact. Yet without fail, the moment I became a full-time youth pastor, right out of college with a paycheck, I started to think about numbers all the time and how many people were showing up to programs! Numbers have their place, because they do represent souls, but by allowing numbers to be my sole measurement for successful ministry, I became consumed by a burden to perform and produce.

Thinking back, it's clear to me how my misplaced focus fueled a sense of competition with others and was rooted in my egocentric desire to succeed and be respected.

> Do we believe our call is to be better than the church next door or to help the church next door become better?

For believers not in formal leadership positions, it would be easy to shrug this off and to claim that as Christians we are not personally guilty of competition that contributes to disunity. It's easier to blame the leaders or put the responsibility on our pastors. But we *all* are part of the body, therefore we all carry a responsibility.

We may also be tempted to say there is a difference between disunity and good old healthy competition. But let's be honest. We have all felt jealousy toward another ministry. At some point we have all compared our ministry to another and felt inadequate, compared our ministry to another and felt superior, or looked at the other churches and ministries in our community and thought, *I have to be better.* The hard truth is that at times in our ministry, we have each taken our focus off of Christ and instead, spent our time, energy, and resources on simply trying to look better than the church next door. When this kind of shift becomes the norm, we stand on the brink of failure in sharing the Gospel and making disciples. Our very mission is in the balance. With leadership also comes a burden to lead toward the unity Christ longs for!

Fueled by egocentric ideas, we tend to see ourselves as individuals rather than as members of a living body. The cultural machine, from birth it seems, teaches that goal number one in life is to get ahead, beat the competition, climb the ladder, and live at the top. It is vital to identify that the cultural trend of competition changes the culture of our churches in many ways down to how we manage time, use money, and strategize marketing. If the culture in a church is that of competition, then profits, finished products, and success will drive our energies. Church, is this what Christ has called us to?

So where does this dominant cultural trait of competition come from? It actually has its roots in the ideas we hold about ourselves. Our individualism is the root problem and the antidote is interdependence. It looks like this:

Root problem: individualism = creates competition
Root solution: interdependence = creates completion
and unity

In the same way that there is a positive turning point for the "egocentric self" (if we use the ability to think about ourselves for self-evaluation and growth rather than selfishness), there is a positive turning point for the cultural trend of competition. Economists consider that competition actually *regulates* individualism (or egocentrism) in a market.[18] We live in communities with other people and their mere presence diminishes an individual's tendency to act for their own benefit at all times. In other words, in the marketplace we are accountable to those around us. Totally egocentric and selfish individuals are pushed aside in a competitive market, which regulates individualism.

> The biblical call is not for competition, but completion.

The biblical call is not for competition, but completion. In the same way that a puzzle comes together or the parts of a human body complete one another, Paul calls individuals and churches to strive toward this state of interdependence and completion (more on this in chapter 3). In 1 Corinthians, Paul goes on to reprimand tendencies toward pride and competition: "The eye cannot say to the hand, 'I don't need you!' And the head cannot say to the feet, 'I don't need you!'" (1 Corinthians 12:21 NIV). This idea came to life one particular summer when several churches in our area wanted to serve the downtown district through painting, landscaping, trash pickup, and minor construction. One church had the trailers full of tools, another leader had key relationships with the city to organize work sites, and another leader specialized in mobilizing others to join the mission and recruiting teams of volunteers. Everyone offered their strengths, resulting in countless service hours, smiles on the faces of volunteers and recipients, and a face-lift for a community. The key is knowing who you are and what your role is in the function of the body. We must be willing to analyze our community-wide strategies and weigh our motives so that our focus is on how to serve well rather than on trying to outperform other parts of the body.

Our task is to realize the cultural influences impacting our decision making. Competition, freedom, and choice have their value, but not when it keeps us from serving together in the Body of Christ.

Competition Is Not a New Struggle

This modern-day struggle of competition, however, is not new. This struggle was very real when Jesus showed up on the scene. Consider His Hebrew context. Within this patriarchal system, one of the most prestigious community positions was that of the rabbi. Young children in Hebrew culture would transition through different levels of education, with only the best of the best promoted to the next level. The highest level was that of a talmidim, or "disciple."[19] After much preparation, a talmidim would request to follow a rabbi, and if the request was granted, the rabbi would say, "Come, follow me," meaning, *I think you have what it takes to be just like me*. This was a huge honor (and commitment). And it also caused competition among groups of disciples. It was a human system—there was rivalry. In fact, when we open the Gospel of John we see this rivalry clearly. Competition crept in and jealousy found its foothold.

John the Baptist was followed by a group of his own talmidim. At one point when John was baptizing people at Aenon, just west of the Jordan River, his disciples took notice of something. John 3 tells us that John's disciples came to him and said: "Rabbi, he who was with you across the Jordan, to whom you bore witness— look, he is baptizing, *and all are going to him*" (John 3:26 ESV).

I imagine it went something like: "Hey, we have really low turnout today. I wonder what's going on. Isaac, did you remember to post on social media about the baptism service today?"

"Yeah, I did . . . it's probably the holiday weekend."

"Wait a minute, no look, everyone is going over *there.*"

John's disciples came to him concerned that they were losing all their followers to another rabbi. Competition.

The next verse shows us how healthy leaders handle competition in the Church. John's simple and profound response was amazing: "He must increase, but I must decrease" (John 3:30 ESV).

Wow. There is a lesson of massive importance here for Christian leaders in John's response. His humility and settled sense of trust in the Lord is incredible. Through his response, John showed deep understanding of his identity and purpose. Only when you know whose you are and what your purpose is will you be able to serve God without concern for the normal pressures of the world.

We see a similar interaction from Paul in 1 Corinthians:

> I appeal to you, brothers and sisters, in the name of our Lord Jesus Christ, that all of you agree with one another in what you say and that there be no divisions among you, but that you be perfectly united in mind and thought. My

brothers and sisters, some from Chloe's household have informed me that there are quarrels among you. What I mean is this: One of you says, "I follow Paul"; another, "I follow Apollos"; another, "I follow Cephas"; still another, "I follow Christ." Is Christ divided? Was Paul crucified for you? Were you baptized in the name of Paul?

1 Corinthians 1:10–13 NIV

This is a quintessential drop-the-mic moment. Paul effectively says: "You've lost sight of the big picture! What are you doing quarreling about who you follow and what group you are a part of? Complete one another perfectly for Christ and remember the mission: share *Christ* crucified, and Him alone."

This is a wake-up call moment for the church in Corinth. Paul was fed up with them! Just a couple chapters later in 1 Corinthians 3, he drills them about being spiritual infants because of the jealousy and quarreling among them. It is because of their division and competition that Paul calls them worldly and not people who live by the Spirit.

This was all massively important to Paul—he spent a lot of time talking about it, and not just in 1 Corinthians. It's no wonder that in the same letter (1 Corinthians 12, 13), Paul gives a compelling exposition on spiritual gifts: how they come from *one* spirit, and then he gives a moving metaphor of how we are many parts of *one* body. It is no coincidence that this all culminates in the epic and powerful poem about what true love is. We must see this poem on love in the context of the case Paul was building in the letter about unity. Re-read this poem with the backdrop of a church that was competing and quarreling: "Love is patient and kind; love does not envy or boast;

it is not arrogant or rude. It does not insist on its own way; it is not irritable or resentful; it does not rejoice at wrongdoing, but rejoices with the truth. Love bears all things, believes all things, hopes all things, endures all things. Love never ends" (1 Corinthians 13:4–8 ESV).

Just because this struggle has been around a while, it offers us no excuse to throw our hands up and say, "That's just the way things are." Instead, all the more reason we need to do something about it!

So, how should the Church today respond to this dominant cultural trait of competition?

HOW DOES THIS PLAY OUT IN THE CHURCH?

I was six years old when my family left Argentina. Standing on a steep mechanical escalator at the Ezeiza Airport in Buenos Aires, I watched my extended family grow smaller as the distance increased between us. My *abuela*, aunts, uncles, and cousins stood in a huddle, solemnly waving farewell as I clutched my father's hand.

The big move came about after my father accepted a position at Scripture Union. It required that my family move from Buenos Aires, Argentina, to Philadelphia. *The United States is going to be a very exciting place...*" or so our parents told me, possibly exaggerating the benefits of our move to soften our transition.

Once settled in our new home, my family attended a non-denominational church in Springfield, Pennsylvania. On a visit to my home church much later while I was in college, I looked across the street and realized, for the first time ever, it seemed, that there was another church right across the street! It took me almost fifteen years to realize that across the street from the church where I grew up there was another vital member of the Body of Christ. I had to ask myself, *Why was I not taught to care about this while growing up?*

With my parents in vocational ministry, I spent much of my time in ministry contexts: on mission trips, in churches of all shapes and sizes, and I've attended most of the major ministry and leadership conferences, even choosing a Christian college and doing a ministry major. In all that time, even in the multicultural contexts where I found myself, I cannot remember unity ever being emphasized as a central keystone to the Gospel.

The point is: unity is barely ever talked about today by followers of Christ. Despite the great emphasis Jesus and Paul placed on it, our mainstream Christian culture is largely devoid of this message. N. T. Wright points out that if you pick up a volume of Pauline theology, most authors will exhaust topics of God, sin, man, Jesus, and the resurrection, but never or rarely unity. Typically, toward the back of the book, there is a chapter on the Church and as a small subsection to that, some commentary on the unity of the Church. Wright further expounds that this is our Western projection on Paul. But if we read Paul in his true context, we'd see that the unity of the Church is absolutely central and at the very heart of the Gospel.[20]

In December 2017 I had the privilege of sitting down with N. T. Wright in St. Andrews, Scotland, to talk about unity in the global Church. As one of the world's leading New Testament and Pauline scholars, Wright shared how he finds it curious that fans of Paul laud him so much for justification, yet ignore his great emphasis on unity. Wright pointed out that Paul talks about unity in *every* one of his books, but the same is not true about justification.[21]

Unlike Paul, we don't talk about unity much at the theological level or in mainstream teaching to young Christians. The church gravitates toward programmatic ministries like evangelism, discipleship, and community service. But we work against ourselves when we do not remove the disunity that will hinder those endeavors. Imagine if we started to teach young believers about the power of a *murmurating* Church! In just a few years, we would have a whole generation of leaders who would embrace and work out a vision of a unified body.

Paul wrote to the Corinthians that "The human body has many parts, but the many parts make up only one body. So it is with the body of Christ. Some of us are Jews, some are Gentiles, some are slaves, and some are free. But we have all been baptized into Christ's body by one Spirit, and we have all received the same Spirit" (1 Corinthians 12:12–13 NLT). Today, this verse might read: "Some of us are Methodist, some are Hispanic, some are Presbyterian, some are African American, some are Baptist, some don't know what they are. But we have all been baptized into Christ." This is a call for completion! Hallelujah!

The *ideas* and *culture* that influence our current reality impact both the spiritual and physical unity of the Church. The tangible and intangible. Meaning, the buildings we construct, the outreach programs we develop, the thought patterns we keep, the language we use, and the feelings we nurture. Without diverse influences, we remain caged in our groups.

For the first eighteen hundred years of church history, almost no one viewed the church as a multitude of small, separate, and independently unrelated flocks.[22] The pendulum has swung in the opposite direction as evidenced by the thousands of denominations worldwide. We now have such a strong history of division that most Christians have a very vague understanding of unity.[23]

Deep in your bones, we hope you feel by now that something is not quite right with the lack of unity in the church. Although there are flare-ups of collaboration, our flock remains largely fragmented. God has given us a wonderful gift in His love, His grace, and His mission, but we can't seem to see past the wrapping paper. We have limited our vision, and, like two brothers on Christmas morning fighting over presents, we can't comprehend how the actual gift is so much bigger than the box. The key to opening this gift of God's love and experiencing it fully is *unity*. The end result will be a gift that far exceeds any expectation we may have.

We must not lose heart at our current reality, because identifying our dissent, disunity, and quarrels may also become the gauge that tells us there is a problem. The negative factors can be used to our advantage when we see them as indicators of a dysfunctional condition in the system.

To move past the ideas and culture that keep us divided, we must repent and have an increasing identification with Christ's Church rather than our in-group or any other dividing line. This is what Leary, quoting Maslow, calls "incorporating others into our *self*"—the more we integrate others into being a part of "us" the more we respond to others' experiences as if they were our very own.[24] This is vital to the health of the Church!

When something is a part of *us*, we like it more. In the same way, when we see others as part of us we begin to treat them like we treat ourselves.[25] This sure sounds like something Jesus already taught: "Love your neighbor as yourself" (Romans 13:9 NIV). We knew what the commandment was, but now we know how to do it: incorporate your neighbor into your own identity and love them as you love yourself.

The crucial test to our faithfulness to Christ's vision for unity will be our willingness to see others win! When you are genuinely happy when others are promoted, honored, and recognized, that will be the marker of maturity beyond individualism and competition. When someone else tells you a story about something amazing that happened to them and you don't get a sinking feeling, worrying about why those experiences aren't happening to you, you will know you are not operating in the worldly mind-set, but in the spirit of 1 Corinthians 12: "If one member suffers, all suffer together; if one member is honored, all rejoice together" (1 Corinthians 12:26 ESV).

Church, we were designed to murmurate, and it is time to break down the negative ideas and cultural influences that keep us in our divided reality. Unity is a daunting task, but when you finally embrace it and call others to join you in fulfilling Christ's mission, it will be so very rewarding!

Chapter 3

God's Vision for Unity

With all wisdom and understanding, he made known to us the mystery of his will . . . to bring unity to all things in heaven and on earth under Christ.

—Ephesians 1:8–10 NIV

With an excruciating death at His doorstep, Jesus' thoughts were on unity.

Close your eyes for a second and picture Jesus in the final hours before going to the cross. As you read the passage of Scripture below, take a moment and place yourself in the following scene:

You are one of the disciples with Jesus. You begin to nervously pick at the calluses on your hands because Jesus' serious and burdened countenance puts you on edge. You've never seen Him like this before. In addition to that, you just finished an intensely emotional supper with Jesus where He washed your feet. There seems to be a shift in the mood among the group. Something serious is happening. Now, Jesus, your

rabbi, begins to pray to the Father. As you listen, your heart
is softened and filled with praise as you hear the passionate
prayer of your Lord:

> I am coming to you now, but I say these things while I am
> still in the world, so that they may have the full measure
> of my joy within them ... My prayer is not that you take
> them out of the world but that you protect them from the
> evil one. They are not of the world, even as I am not of
> it. Sanctify them by the truth; your word is truth. As you
> sent me into the world, I have sent them into the world ...
> My prayer is not for them alone. I pray also for those who
> will believe in me through their message, that all of them
> may be one, Father, just as you are in me and I am in you.
> May they also be in us so that the world may believe that
> you have sent me. I have given them the glory that you
> gave me, that they may be one as we are one—I in them
> and you in me —so that they may be brought to complete
> unity. Then the world will know that you sent me and
> have loved them even as you have loved me.
>
> John 17:13–23 NIV

Wow. You feel the weight of the spoken truth: unity is mission critical for the world to see Jesus as Lord! Overwhelmed
by the power and depth of Jesus' prayer, you, too, begin to
pray, now echoing Jesus' words: "Father, make us one just as
you are one. May the whole world come to know you through
our unity. Father, through our love for one another and united
efforts, may the world experience your love. Amen! Amen!"
What a powerful moment that must have been. In this

prayer, Jesus lays out His strategy for the best way to declare His lordship to the world: the unity of His followers. Without question, establishing the vision to cultivate *creative tension* begins in John 17. Jesus' greatest hope and vision is clear: **through our unity, the world will know God.**

As many have said, a person's final words are sometimes the most important. In Jesus' final (and longest) documented prayer, He sums up His teaching and ministry. His prayer is not just an individual prayer or a sentimental look at His life's work. This prayer is a vision for what is to come: the oneness of His Church. Jesus spent so much of his time teaching in parables and figurative speech—sometimes creating more questions than answers. But here, in the last hours of His life, in His farewell speech of sorts, Jesus reveals a vision for the unleashing of His kingdom and mission of the Church.

Think about it. His last thoughts and prayers could have been about *anything*, and He chose unity. It's like the teacher saying, "Of everything I taught, this will definitely be on the test."

This is the core idea of our manifesto: if individual Christians catch Jesus' vision for unity and apply the Murmuration principles with the help of the Holy Spirit, we will move away from division and become the most captivating, exotic, and powerful collective force for good in history.

Maybe you are like Mike and me and you have an intuition that as the Church, followers of Christ are not reaching our fullest potential. Maybe you have a voice in your spirit pointing to something bigger, a greater design for what His Church could be. Well, we are here to confirm that voice. That is the very Spirit echoing the Word of God, calling us to our true design. Calling us to function as one dynamic body with baffling efficiency. Calling us to complete one another to produce the God-sized results for the kingdom that Jesus prayed for.

This chapter is dedicated to showing the biblical passion and vision for unity. The rest of the ideas in this book will never carry the urgency and importance we need unless we first understand *why this matters so much to God*. We will never do the hard work that pursuing unity requires in our personal lives until we understand how vital unity is to our mission. Come and see possibly a fresh angle on God, the Gospel, the Church, and your role in the beautiful story.

A FOUNDATION FOR A SKYSCRAPER

The foundation for the preeminence of unity in the Christian community runs deep. In fact, it would be impossible to overemphasize the importance of unity in the story of God as shared with us in the Scriptures. Entire libraries could be written about it, not only because of the priority it holds in the Word of God, but because as we will explore, unity is central to the very essence of God. In many ways, we've missed how important unity is to God and the Gospel. We do not have the space to explore this in great depth, but the following sequence of ideas will at least provide a framework for the biblical source of this passion and vision:

- Everything God does *begins* in unity
- Everything God does *multiplies* unity
- Jesus *prayed* for YOUnity
- Everything we do must *originate in unity and multiply unity*

EVERYTHING GOD DOES BEGINS IN UNITY

When God set out to tell His story, He did not begin by revealing Himself as a single person, but rather as an imaginative community of creativity. Right from the beginning, in the creation story of Genesis, God describes His debut as a divine family at work—a family that loves, contributes, and becomes something powerful in their unity.

The first chapter of Genesis tells us that "In the beginning God created the heavens and earth. Now the earth was formless and empty. Darkness was over the surface of the deep, and the spirit of God was hovering over the waters. And God said, let there be light and there was light" (Genesis 1:1–3 NIV).

Notice, in the context of the whole Bible, that there are three key players in this passage: God the Father as the creator, the Spirit of God hovering over the waters, and finally in verse 3, God spoke. The Word. Jesus Himself, the light of the world present at creation. All three members are there dancing, working, moving, creating, and can we daresay, murmurating with the other members of the Godhead—in perfect community.

In this beautiful creation project, the three different "personalities" in the Godhead were one in essence and purpose. And as the clay took shape, it was clearly molded by many hands: "Let *us* make man in *our* image" (Genesis 1:26 ESV, emphasis added). In His limitless wisdom, power, and love, God reveals Himself to us as the Trinity.

Fast-forward to another pivotal moment in the Bible where we see this divine family at work again. In Matthew 3, we read Jesus' baptism story:

Then Jesus went from Galilee to the Jordan River to be baptized by John. But John tried to talk him out of it. "I am the one who needs to be baptized by you," he said, "so why are you coming to me?" But Jesus said, "It should be done, for we must carry out all that God requires." So John agreed to baptize him. After his baptism, as Jesus came up out of the water, the heavens were opened and he saw the Spirit of God descending like a dove and settling on him. And a voice from heaven said, "This is my dearly loved Son, who brings me great joy."

Matthew 3:13–17 NLT

Just like at creation, God the Father is present, speaking from heaven. The Holy Spirit descends as a dove, hovering again over water, and of course Jesus is there, the embodiment of the Word of God. But now, the scene looks very different. There is chaos again, but it's a different type of chaos that needs forming and redemption. At first, this cosmic community gave order to creation, but in *this* baptism scene, they are *reordering* creation. This moment of Jesus' baptism was God's announcement that the Messiah had come, marking the launch of Christ's ministry. Not only was it a critical symbol for the death and resurrection that Christ would soon experience, but also an echo to the Genesis story. The old was passing away and *new creation* was about to spring forth.

God's initial work of creation originated in unity and God's relaunching of new creation also began in unity. Everything God does originates in Unity.

EVERYTHING GOD DOES MULTIPLIES UNITY

God's work always begins from a place of unity, and His work also *generates* unity. Between God and man. Between creation and God. Between Jew and Gentile. Between neighbors, cultures, socioeconomic class, or nationalistic divides.

With this understanding, Paul's great declaration on God's design for unity in his letter to the Ephesians makes more sense:

> He made known to us the mystery of His will ... that is, the summing up of all things in Christ, things in the heavens and things on the earth.
>
> Ephesians 1:9–10 NASB

Or:

> With all wisdom and understanding, he made known to us the mystery of his will according to his good pleasure, which he purposed in Christ, to be put into effect when the times reach their fulfillment—to bring unity to all things in heaven and on earth under Christ.
>
> Ephesians 1:8–10 NIV

Consider these passages for a moment and let the truth hit you. In Christ, God revealed the mystery of His will, which is to bring unity to all things in heaven and earth.

The weight of this demands an expansion of how we define and understand the Gospel. It demands an expansion of how we live out being the people of God.

Stories from the book of Acts also show us that God's work multiplies unity. In so many places throughout the book, powerful moves of God are associated with the believers being of one heart and mind. Then in Acts 10, a pivotal moment for the Church occurs. It was a moment when God multiplied unity across seemingly irreconcilable lines. This is the story when Cornelius, a Roman officer, invited Peter to his house. This is not a casual Sunday afternoon gathering—the invitation itself would have broken cultural norms. Jews were not even allowed to enter the homes of Gentiles. But now, God was on the move reproducing unity, and tilling the soil in their hearts through the visions He had given to Peter and Cornelius. When Peter obeyed and moved into unity, crossing Jew and Gentile lines, this opened the door for the Holy Spirit to move, and the entire centurion's household gave their lives to Jesus.

The whole point of Christ's work was to reconcile that which was pulled apart. God is looking for opportunities to multiply unity, because work done in unity among the people of God releases the power of God.

JESUS PRAYED FOR YOUNITY

Jesus' prayer in John 17 is so intimate that you almost feel as though you're overhearing something you are not supposed to hear. But although the relationship between Jesus and the Father is intimate, it is not designed to be exclusive.[1]

In His final wishes, Jesus asks for three things in the John 17 prayer. First, Jesus asks that the Father protect and sanctify the disciples. Second, He prays for you and me! He prayed that all the other "believers" that come after the original twelve disciples would be *one*: you and me. Lastly, Jesus prays that the whole world would come to know the Father through the unity of the believers. Jesus' radical prayer speaks to the heart of what our fellowship is designed to be.

It comes down to humility, the same humility that Christ portrayed when He willingly offered His life. Christ did not exalt Himself, so God exalted Him. That is how we must now serve others. With any situation where unity is at risk, run it through the Philippians 2 filter.

It seems the early believers caught a vision of this unity, but it was not always easy for them to remain unified. That is why Paul had to continually teach them the key to living in it:

So if there is any encouragement in Christ, any comfort from love, any participation in the Spirit, any affection and sympathy, complete my joy by being of the same mind, having the same love, being in full accord and of one mind. Do nothing from selfish ambition or conceit, but in humility count others more significant than yourselves. Let each of you look not only to his own interests, but also to the interests of others. Have this mind among yourselves, which is yours in Christ Jesus, who, though he was in the form of God, did not count equality with God a thing to be grasped, but emptied himself, by taking the form of a servant, being born in the likeness of men. And being found in human form, he humbled himself by becoming obedient to the point of death, even death on a cross. Therefore God has highly exalted him and bestowed on him the name that is above every name, so that at the name of Jesus every knee should bow, in heaven and on earth and under the earth, and every tongue confess that Jesus Christ is Lord, to the glory of God the Father.

Philippians 2:1–11 ESV

Jesus did not achieve unity in His short life on earth. But He did win the ultimate victory over sin and death and released the Holy Spirit, thus giving us the platform through which to achieve unity. He built the bridge for us to a fellowship with God where unity exists. And now, as Wright says, He has given us the task of implementing His victory.[2]

EVERYTHING WE DO MUST ORIGINATE IN UNITY AND MULTIPLY UNITY

Unity is not optional. The mandate of unity reverberates throughout the entire New Testament. The John 17 prayer only builds on Jesus' words in John 13 where he said that the world will know we are His disciples by our love. As the embodiment of Christ's love to the world, the Church should not only *want* to be like our Lord in all things, but we are called to. If unity matters to God, it better be a priority to us.

> The mandate of unity reverberates throughout the entire New Testament.

A key part of early Church growth strategy was unity. Luke places great emphasis on their "togetherness" (Acts 1:14, Acts 2:46–47, Acts 4:24, 32). This unity was not only of an abstract or spiritual nature, but also a tangible, concrete and visible unity (Galatians 3:28) with solutions to real-world problems.[3] This new community was designed to be the billboard to the world of a new way to be human. Theologian Padilla weaves the New Testament message together beautifully:

> Paul states that . . . the divisions that affect the old human-ity have become irrelevant: "Here there cannot be Gen-tile and Jew, circumcised or uncircumcised, barbarian, Scythian slave, free man, but Christ is all and in all." Race loses its importance because all the believers, whether Jews or Gentiles, belong to the "Israel of God" (Gal. 6:16). Religious background is neither here nor there because "the true circumcision" (Phil. 3:3) is made up of Jews who are Jews inwardly, whose circumcision is "real circumcision . . . a matter of the heart, spiritual and not lit-eral" (Rom. 2:28–29). Social stratifications are beside the point because in the new humanity the slave becomes his own master's "beloved brother" (Philem. v.15); the slave is called to serve the Lord and not humankind (Col. 3:22) and the free person is to live as one who has a Master in heaven (Col. 4:11) . . . the only thing that matters is that "Christ is all and in all." Those who have been baptized "into one body" (1 Cor. 12:13) are members of a commu-nity in which the differences that separate people in the world have become obsolete.[4]

The big picture Gospel narrative here tells us that God is the ultimate reconciler. He brings things together.

N. T. Wright points out that unity is at "the heart of Paul's ecclesiology" and that in Romans 15:7–13, at the climax of the letter to the Romans, Paul insists on the united worship of the multicultural church.[5] In all of Paul's letters to the early church, the message is overwhelmingly clear that spiritual unity *and* visible unity in Christ are essential parts of the Gospel.[6] However, we've missed the mission-altering truth that without unity, the Church is incapable of fully implementing the victory that Christ sacrificed so much to accomplish. Now is the time to see afresh what the Church could be. Now is the time to imitate God and originate our work in unity and multiply unity through our work.

> Without unity, the Church is incapable of fully implementing the victory that Christ sacrificed so much to accomplish.

WHAT KIND OF UNITY?

Today, the word "unity" can mean different things to different people, so it is important to clearly define the unity Jesus desires for His Church. Astoundingly, the unity Jesus prays for is the same unity that exists in the Trinity. Literally.

Jesus believes we can be as united as He is with the Father and the Holy Spirit.

His prayer was so bold because He knew the heavy work He was about to do. Jesus knew that He was about to unlock the door that would give each of us access into the fellowship of the divine family.

The theology of a Triune God is central to the Christian faith. Put simply, the doctrine states that God is one being who is made up of three co-equal and co-eternal Persons: the Father, Son, and

> Jesus believes we can be as united as He is with the Father and the Holy Spirit.

Holy Spirit. In other words, the Trinity is not just a team of three individuals cooperating around a common goal—they are completely and wholly one.

The word "trinity" actually means "tri-unity" and although the word "trinity" does not actually appear in the Scriptures, the concept is clearly there throughout the Scriptures.

Dr. Wayne Grudem's words seem to clarify and confuse all at the same time, saying that God eternally exists as "three persons, Father, Son and Holy Spirit. Each person is fully God, and there is one God."[7] Okay, got it. No, Wait. What?

The idea of the Trinity can be daunting, but one of the beautiful things about it is that we will never fully understand it. And that is okay. That might make you cringe, but it points to the mysterious, untamed, and unpredictable power of our Lord.

THE COSMIC DANCE

So, if the Godhead is truly three in one, what then does it look like when three personalities of equal power collide? The answer is found in one word: perichoresis. It's a Greek term originally meaning to "go around," but think more in terms of "dancing" instead of "avoiding." In the Christian faith, it has taken on a meaning to refer to the interactions that happen when Father, Son, and Holy Spirit live and move together.

Some things can be explained better with art rather than with words, and this certainly applies to the theology of perichoresis.

In Celtic culture, they are experts in making interwoven

Celtic knot (Oleg Zhevelev—stock.adobe.com)

knots like the one pictured here. It is an amazing symbol of interconnectedness and unity with no beginning or end. Ian Bradley says: "The intertwining ribbons of the Celtic knot represent in simple and graphic terms the doctrine of *perichoresis*— the mutual interpenetration of Father, Son and Holy Spirit."[8] The word connotes the mutual inter-relationship and inter- dwelling of the Godhead and speaks to deep intimacy, fellow- ship, movement and oneness of the three members.

Some theologians even call it a *dance*.

Could it be a Murmuration of cosmic proportions happen- ing among the most powerful being in the universe?

In the Christian faith, the triangle is one of the oldest symbols for God and the Trinity (it also happens to be the strongest shape in nature). A deeper look at the symbols we use can open up our understanding of the person of God. Today, we've enhanced the triangle with a Celtic remix known as the triquetra. It has

Trinity knot (Lucas Ramirez)

become the most popular symbol for representing the Trinity. This shape is saturated with meaning and imagery. The three equal arches each represent one person of the Godhead and point to the equality of the Father, Son, and Holy Spirit. Also, the union of the arches represents the union of the Godhead. Furthermore, their continuous form symbolizes the eternal nature of the relationship, and the interwoven design of the triquetra denotes the indivisibility of the Trinity. There is so much in one symbol!

With this deeper view of Father, Son, and Holy Spirit, we look again at John 17 and see Jesus' prayer against this backdrop. Jesus asks that we, the Church, may be just as united as the Trinity! That is not just surface-level unity. The unity that Christ wants for the church is this: **unity is when all followers of Jesus realize their interconnectedness and pursue the oneness as seen in the Triune God in order to become one with God and each other—for His glory and the expansion of His kingdom.**

This unity allows each member to remain an individual

while contributing to the collective whole. It grows a community marked by love, generosity, and grace; a community where our relationships are never on the negotiating table. This is the dance, the perichoresis, or *Murmuration*, that God deeply desires for the Church.

A HUNDRED BIRDS DON'T MAKE A MEGA BIRD; THEY MAKE A FLOCK

The Murmuration vision is *not* to dissolve churches and create one mega church, or to have one organization lead the way. Further, the goal is not to house everyone under one central authority. History has already tried this (through the World Council of Churches, the Vatican, and others). We have struggled to create the authentic united movements that God designed us for. It is time to take a fresh approach.

The call is for an emergent movement where believers start fighting for unity in their communities. It is a call to see ourselves as a true body with many diverse parts that can come together for collective citywide strategies in our corner of the world. It looks like sharing resources outside of our typical in-group in order to feed the hungry or preach the good news of the cross. We don't lose our individual identity in this vision, because each church and individual has their own vital role in the community. The goal is not to become one mega bird. The goal is to learn to fly in unison.

Many thanks are owed to those who have worked tirelessly in the ecumenical movement. We stand on their shoulders. Much has been accomplished in the last one hundred plus years since the Edinburgh World Mission Conference of 1910 (widely held to be the start of the modern-day ecumenical movement). The conference hosted twelve hundred delegates from many different church denominations and mission societies.

Although we have come a long way, much of the ecumenical work of the last century has been at higher organizational levels. For example, in the early 2000s a bilateral dialogue was established between the Presbyterian and Episcopal traditions. These ecumenical talks resulted in the 2009 agreement that encouraged joint ministry and collaboration. Even earlier than that, in 1960 Pope John XXIII established the *Secretariat for Promoting Christian Unity* (now called the Pontifical Council for Promoting Christian Unity), which exists to strengthen relationships with other Christians for unity. These conversations at the top levels of leadership are valuable and important because they contribute to the needed structural changes, but how much have everyday believers felt the daily impact of these high-level agreements?

There have been many fruitful exchanges; however, what we need today is more than organizational declarations. Church history has demonstrated that Christianity has not been served well by high organizational structures. The Church becomes most alive as it emerges in small groups. The power of the Church is not in its organizational form, but in the people and their actions.

For the many pieces of the puzzle to come together, it will require a bottom-up initiative with the emphasis on *local interactions*. The movement needs people who are willing to live with differences and learn from one another, people who are willing to have hard conversations across a coffee table rather than on social media comment streams.

We need a groundswell that is organic and local.

This vision for a local movement, however, comes with a warning: a local and decentralized movement can lose vital historical and traditional roots if we hyper-fixate on the current micro or ethnocentric context. The Church is a *global* community and we must never forget we are part of a greater multiethnic and multigenerational fellowship. Without a global perspective, we run the risk of losing an important layer of accountability that we need in order to stay biblically based. Our inability to find a balance may be why no single proposal for unity has become wildly successful.[9]

WHAT THE VISION IS NOT

First, unity is not uniformity. The biblical vision will not express itself as uniformity of theology, music, or culture. We will not always agree with everyone on strategy, preferences, or thought. On the essentials, there must be absolute unity, but when it comes to secondary doctrinal issues, we must engage others with love and humility. Getting everyone to think and act the same way is *not* possible and it should not be our goal. Consider the basics of artistic design from art expert Patrick Frank:

> Unity and variety are complementary concerns. Unity is the appearance or condition of oneness. In design, unity describes the feeling that all the elements in a work belong together and make up a coherent and harmonious whole... When a work of art has unity, we feel that any change would diminish its quality. Variety, on the

other hand, provides diversity. Variety acts to counter unity. The sameness of too much unity is boring, and the diversity of uncontrolled variety is chaotic, but a balance between unity and variety creates life.[10]

We become more beautiful with the balance of unity and variety!

Second, unity is not merely in our hearts and spirits—it is physical and visible too. The unity Jesus prayed for was not just for unity's sake. The greater purpose for unity is for the world to see God through our love and united missional efforts. The power in our service as we clothe the naked and love the outcasts is exponential if we can show unlikely groups of people serving shoulder to shoulder. It is not merely the act of love, self-sacrifice, and generosity that will catch the world's attention, but even more so, *who* is doing it together. Looking again to the world of art, visual unity demands harmony between many items *that become apparent to the eye*.[11] The unity in the Church has remained largely spiritual, abstract, and invisible. It must now permeate our minds, hearts, *and* hands to become a tangible and apparent expression.

Third, unity does not come at the sacrifice of the purity of the Church. Theologians talk about the tension that exists between the "purity" of the church and the "unity" of the church created by believers' passion for truth and their interpretation of Scripture. In our culture, we like to make lists of what a pure Church looks like, listing things such as biblical doctrine, proper use of sacraments, genuine worship, and spiritual power in ministry, among others.[12] Consider also Ben Witherington's words: "Protestantism has tended to hold up

Truth, with a capital T, while intonating unity with a lower-case u . . . On the other hand, Catholicism and Orthodoxy have held up Unity with a capital U, and at least from the Protestant viewpoint this has been at the expense of Truth."[13]

While this conversation regarding the purity or unity of the Church has merit, the dialogue is operating from a wrong premise because *unity actually contributes to the purity of the church.* This is not an either/or scenario, because unity and purity do not stand opposed as if on two ends of a spectrum. We'll touch on this more in chapter 9.

Fourth, a vision for unity does not mean we cannot make strong belief statements. Searching for unity is not the same thing as searching for compromise. This is not a movement for tolerance of a universalistic approach to faith. Jesus did not say "Be unified and just let everyone believe whatever they want" or "Be careful not to make any strong belief statements that offend other people." Instead, His message was "I am the way the truth and the life. No one comes to the Father except through me" (John 14:6 NIV). His words and teachings were strong and it is okay for ours to be too—as long as they are soaked in a waterfall of humility and love. If you can't handle dialogue and instead always need to debate or push an agenda, then, and I say this respectfully, please keep your mouth shut. You are hindering the unity of the Spirit.

Fifth, murmurating as followers of Christ does not mean we have to work together on everything all the time. Even in the Murmuration there are times the flock separates, *but only when it makes strategic sense for the larger mission.* This usually occurs when a predator dives into the flock during an attack. The starlings then quickly regroup and come back together, deeply committed to the flock. The *why* behind our separation is the critical difference between God-glorifying movements that reflect our Lord and human decisions that grieve the Spirit.

Finally, unity is achievable, but it is not easily attainable. Protecting the oneness of the Spirit is not a skip through the park. This is the stuff of guts and glory and probably one of the hardest fields we may plow, but the harvest will be immeasurable. Through the Scriptures, nature, and the revelation of His Son, God has shown us how we can operate like a flock. We have already been invited into the fellowship of the Trinity through Christ and have full access to this same love and community with God and with our neighbor. But we have to be all-in for His vision. If not, then it is just behavior modification.

Murmurations cause people to look *up*. The Scriptures are clear, that through the unity of the Church, the world, too, will look up to encounter God. It is time for followers of Christ to murmurate and cause others to look up to God! It is time that we boost the profile of unity in our leadership circles, our seminaries, in our job descriptions, and in our mission statements.

Do you want to be part of a global ripple effect where the world knows Christ as King through a Church operating within its design? You can! It begins with originating our work in unity and ensuring that our work multiplies unity.

With the biblical vision of unity and our current reality in the backdrop, hopefully we have the creative tension that our movement needs to propel us forward. Our *why* and *what* now need a *how*. How do we make the vision a reality? Part 2 will unveil the Murmuration principles to uncover precisely *how* we build unity here and now.

Part Two

UNVEILING THE MURMURATION PRINCIPLES

In part 1, we established God's design for unity and explored our current fragmented state as the Body of Christ. This hopefully gave us a framework for generating the creative tension and urgency we need to raise the importance of unity in the Church.

In part 2, we dive into the Murmuration, learning about the wonders of the phenomenon and draw out seven principles that will unleash collective movement in the Body of Christ!

Chapter 4

Principle 1: Seven Influential Neighbors

The enemy knows that when we are united, we are unstoppable for the mission of God.

—Craig Groeschel[1]

The spectacular maneuvers of the starlings ripple through the air like rolling waves that caress the sky, each bird somehow lost in the madness yet retaining their value as an individual of the larger whole. Through this extraordinary display, onlookers are left stupefied with a pressing question: How can the starlings react so fast and move with such fluency and finesse?

Let me put their speed in context. The average human reaction time is 194 milliseconds. Not bad, right? We can get as fast as 107 milliseconds when we can anticipate movement in chorus-line situations like "the wave" at a stadium or the Rockettes at Radio City Music Hall. Birds, however, operate on another level. In lab tests, scientist Wayne Potts discovered that a bird's average startle reaction time is 38 milliseconds.

Pretty fast—that's about five times faster than humans. But it gets even better. When reacting in a Murmuration, the birds' reaction time more than doubles in speed: down to a staggering 15 milliseconds![2]

Scientists unraveled the mystery of the starlings' record-breaking speed by studying the flight patterns of birds within a Murmuration. At first, the hypothesis proposed that the birds were reacting to their neighbors within a certain radius. They imagined that each bird might be the center of their own sphere and would bank right or left based on the motion of any bird within a specific distance, possibly reacting to the birds within ten or five feet of them.

Although their research ended up disproving their hypothesis, it revealed something much more interesting: in a Murmuration, starlings continually respond to their seven closest neighbors at any given time.[3] It is not a matter of distance, but of relationship. They are on nonstop alert, watching while in flight, and basing their median speed on that of their seven closest neighbors. Even more amazing is that by their awareness of the seven neighbors, they become simultaneously aware of the movements of the entire flock. By relating well to the few around them, they develop an interconnectivity to the larger body.

The key to their incredible reaction time of fifteen milliseconds is relationships. In fact, many bird species are highly social, breeding and bathing together, or roosting in congregations. According to Jennifer Ackerman, birds argue, cheat, kidnap, give gifts, tease, share, kiss, and teach their young. Some scientists even suggest certain species have social lives nearly as complex as our own: showing jealousy or quarreling and then making amends.[4]

The starlings in particular are extremely social. They gather food together in small social groups during the day and then roost in massive quantities at night. There are huge payoffs to being social. For example, the birds don't have to relearn how to open nuts or take risks with predators or poisonous foods. They can stay warm together, share resources, and watch their neighbors to imitate their behavior. And they leverage their relationships to murmurate, showcasing their massive display of power and speed.

So why do their relationships create speed? Because relationships allow for *anticipation.* The speed in the formation is a direct result of anticipating and predicting the movements of their seven closest neighbors. Starlings understand the power of relationship and value what their neighbors offer. Without each starling's awareness and commitment to the seven other starlings around them, the Murmuration would be impossible.

DESIGNED FOR COMMUNITY

God designed us for relationships too. Everything that God does originates in and multiplies unity. It's part of our very fabric. We are designed for common unity. This was engineered so that we would mirror God and also enjoy the beauty that other people bring into our lives. The enemy works freely in isolation, but in community we propel one another to greater faith and untapped potential.

This community, this fellowship of believers, was not designed to be a single-flavored exclusive group of identical people. As God envisions it, it is a bouquet, bursting with diversity of language, smells, traditions, clothing styles, and music. In Galatians, the whole heart behind the letter is that a Jewish Christian and Gentile Christian should sit at the same table together. As N. T. Wright says, "That's not incidental; it's the main point of the argument."[5] The good news of Christ's renewal work turned the world upside down and brought together what was previously separated. We hear again the echoes: at the center of the Gospel's power is the revolutionary work of uniting that which was divided.

Similarly to the starlings, the common unity among the people of God is not powerful merely because of sheer numbers or diversity in itself. The power lies in the interplay between the individuals and *how* they relate to one another. You could easily fill a room with a crowd of people, but that does not mean you have a Murmuration. **You can unlock the power of the collective only when the individuals within a group commit to meaningful relationships with one another.**

This longing for unity and community is hardwired in our souls. We crave connectivity and meaningful relationships. The hard part is actually finding strong community. Rare are the fellowships that go beyond surface-level niceties and allow for the raw realities of our lives without judgment, gossip, or jealousy. But just because they are rare or difficult does not mean we

> You can unlock the power of the collective only when the individuals within a group commit to meaningful relationships with one another.

cannot pursue them or achieve them. In fact, if we, the people of God, want to see His Kingdom come on earth just as it is in heaven, we must realize that our relationships are one of *the* cornerstones for the expansion of our mission.

When the Scriptures call us to "live in harmony with one another..." and to "be devoted to one another in love. Honor one another above yourselves" (Romans 12:16, Romans 12:10 NIV), it is not for our own benefit. Remember that God is interested in things that also *multiply* unity. His design is for us to leverage the power of the collective to love and reach the world.

Often, we get comfortable with the few relationships we currently have. "I've got enough relationships" we've heard many say. Or "I don't have time" for investing in more relationships. We must ask ourselves, both as individuals and organizations, what incredible opportunities or moves of God have we missed out on because we remain stuck in our bubble or small view of the Body of Christ? Even worse, could it be that we are unknowingly being a roadblock to others when we don't expand our relationships to *anticipate* the movements of other believers around us?

Relationships. The answer sounds almost too simple, doesn't it? It may be simple, but it's certainly not easy. Relationships are hard. They take time. And they are not always full of sunshine. Beyond that, diverse relationships are even harder because we think we'll have to work harder, and we like our comfort zones with people who look like us, think like us, even smell like us.

But the truth is that when we enter into a relationship with someone from a different culture, tradition, or just a different part of the neighborhood, we begin to see the beauty in their differences. Often, we find they are not that different.

When we get to know someone, our awareness and perspective change. Then our entire mental model shifts because in relationship we are no longer outsiders looking in, but rather insiders sharing beautiful stories of what God is doing among us. We become family—brothers and sisters in Christ, no matter the differences in our heritage or background. This is the powerful space where relationships begin to produce *anticipation* for what other parts of the Body are doing in your city.

A firm emphasis on authentic relationships is also how we get away from the *competition* and *individualism* that we talked about in chapter 2. When we befriend someone from across the denominational pew, we begin to appreciate their creativity and see the value of their projects too. If we have a sincere heart, we will desire to see them succeed and multiply, even if it does not benefit us directly.

Investing in relationships with other believers is *the most practical way to begin walking in unity*. We cannot overemphasize this enough. If you get nothing else from this book, do this: begin pursuing diverse and authentic relationships (they can be both personal and professional). Just like the starlings, this will generate the *anticipation* that we need for one another's movements. We simply must know each other if we have any hope at unleashing Christ's vision for unity and the mission of the Church. The challenge rests on you. Go and find your Seven Influential Neighbors.

In these next pages, we will uncover four practical rules to follow to identify your seven closest neighbors:

1. Come to the table
2. Keep it diverse

3. It's a roundtable, not a boardroom

4. Stay at the table

COME TO THE TABLE

Another meeting? Yes, and you'd better stop complaining. Jesus can hear you.

Relationships take time together in the same spaces and at the same table. Step one is initiating, but then you have to show up consistently. Nobody said it had to be a boring table though. It could be the lunch table or a coffee table. Heck, relationships even grow (or dissolve!) at the ping-pong table.

Gathering should feel natural, not forced. It is a time where we learn about one another's lives. We need to gather inside *and* outside of formal meetings. I know what you're thinking: *schedules are already insanely tight.* But with this bigger vision in mind, we need to stop allowing the urgent to dominate the important. If we are serious about our calling to be one body, nothing can replace the face-to-face meeting. *We have to make time for coming together to promote unity!*

Begin by praying. Ask the Lord to show you which individuals He wants to bring together. Don't feel like you have to start with Seven Influential Neighbors right away. You may invite a few and then add more later. No agenda. Just begin with real friendships (don't worry, we'll get to the strategy, too, for you action-oriented folks!). Invite people into relationships with eternal significance—these connections have the possibility of unleashing the mission of the Church!

Whether you are a ministry leader, teacher, lawyer, or

stay-at-home mom, you have the ability to help demolish the dam of disunity! The key is to gather and make sure the meetings bring real value to those who show up. Make sure the time with your Seven Influential Neighbors is relational and intentional. Just showing up means a lot, but if there is no plan for the gathering, people will stop coming. I wouldn't blame them. Yes, relationships are worth it, but in our busy world, we can easily forget how relationships fit into the bigger picture. If the meetings are too long or the group evolves into an unstructured social hour, it will lose its priority in people's schedules.

Bring just the right amount of structure to your gatherings so people know what to expect. You can accomplish this goal by using various elements that keep your gatherings enriching: each person can share their life story, pray together, invite special guest speakers, discuss an article, book, or Scripture. Find whatever works for your group culture and offer everyone a relational, safe, predictable, and intentional environment. At *every* meeting, remind the group why you have gathered and the greater purpose that unity plays in the Church. Whether you choose the ping-pong table or the coffee table, the group has to commit to showing up.

MIKE'S STORY

In my decades of building networks, I've found that there is no pill, quick fix, or logic flow for trust in relationships because of the emotional complexity behind relationships. The key element of trust is developed only when we take the time to build relationships. Unity takes time because trust takes time. It is in relationships that we share the "happy and crappy" of our stories, being intentional inside and outside of meetings. Old school takes new school out for lunch, church connects with para-church, bi-vocational with the full-time leader.

There are times in the life of a community when we are called to step up and raise the bar in our commitment to each other and to the welfare of our communities. That's what happened with a group of youth workers in Kenosha, Wisconsin. This group of leaders was meeting on a monthly basis to pray a little, eat a lot, and plan an event they would do months later. Then tragedy woke them up: a spirit of darkness seemed to hang heavy on one of the local high school campuses. There were a number of suicides in a short period of time. It shook these youth workers to the core. They reassessed what they were doing as a network and became serious about why they were meeting. Prayer became the priority. They began meeting together every Thursday to pray. Quickly, the focus of their prayers centered on the city and on evangelism. They got serious about doing more than social events, and they focused on unity among themselves. The youth workers knew there were differences among them as leaders, but they agreed to put those aside to be on a mission together for Christ. Their partnerships were based on relationships that produced humility and submission to one another, and suddenly the city became a singular mission field for them to reach *together.*

> Then it spread.
>
> Students at the high school campus saw the unity among the youth leaders, and *they* began gathering to pray for their peers at their school. In Kenosha, light broke through the darkness and real lives were saved because a group of youth workers intentionally came to the table.

The Power of Coming to the Table

Consider the psychology and sociology behind the need to physically gather and come to the table with your Seven Influential Neighbors. Getting together with other believers who are different is vital because it creates **shared experiences**. Research shows that a common experience with someone else causes a profound sense of connection with each other, even if the two are quite different. These moments create the "remember when..." memories that are so critical for creating a relational history, and they break down negative *metaperceptions* that we hold (what we think they think about us).[6]

Shared experiences don't just benefit the group, however. Sociologists Boothby, Clark, and Bargh conducted research showing that shared experiences actually amplify the *individual's* experience too.[7] Have you ever noticed that watching a sunset with someone is more meaningful than experiencing it alone? Visiting a new city and traveling are awesome experiences, but those journeys always mean more when they are shared. In God's beautiful design, when we pursue unity and relationship with others, it actually enhances our individual experience too!

Imagine you are a punk-rock motorcycle-riding fifty-year-old evangelist and you just rode your bike to the Grand Canyon. Then up drives a vegan progressive twenty-year-old driving a solar-powered car. When he steps out, the smell of essential oils fills the air. Other than both being human, you two have almost nothing in common. But as you stand at the edge together, looking out over the majestic canyon, you share a moment of awe. However brief, it's a shared experience.

Sociologists tell us that moments like these are powerful connectors. But we typically don't give diverse unity a chance because we don't gather in spaces where shared experiences can happen. We can accomplish this by getting intentional about where we go to church, conferences we attend, and places we shop.

We have to fight for these diverse shared experiences because today, it is harder than ever to experience life with people who are different. Even in our public spaces such as grocery stores, parks, and coffee shops, our communities are more uniform than ever. This is partly evidenced by the fact that in recent years, the number of landslide political races has increased, showing that we have even relocated into regions of homogeneous communities. It is time to expand our circle and come to the table with those who may not be quite like us.

KEEP IT DIVERSE

Have you heard of the *diversity dividend*? Some of the recent research done by the global consulting firm McKinsey shows that companies with more diverse teams significantly outperform their competition.[8] By looking at data sets from 366 public companies from across the world, they found that companies with gender diverse teams financially outperform other companies by 15 percent, and companies with ethnically diverse teams financially outperform less diverse companies by 35 percent! This is the diversity dividend.

In God's economy, our bottom line is not financial profit, but what sort of kingdom dividends have we missed out on because of our sorted, homogeneous, and divided state?

We often miss so much when in our comfortable nests, not realizing we are really in self-made cages that hold us back from erupting into epic Murmurations. If we followed the example of Christ and engaged our diverse neighbors, the results would produce a kingdom dividend that God is expecting with the talents He has given us to steward. Staying in our safe places and fearing the risk of diversity is equivalent to burying our talent and returning it to our master when He returns. "Where is my dividend?" He will ask of us.

Coming to the table is step one, but *who* comes to the table is the next element to consider. Your Seven Influential Neighbors cannot be all identical or there will be little learning. Just like the starlings, one of the main purposes of the connections is that the relationships will influence *you*. This means coming to the table with the humility to see the world through a different lens. And this runs much deeper than just the color of our skin: consider generational, cultural, theological, political, socioeconomic, or gender differences.

In the same way that relationships cannot be forced, it is absolutely critical to not force diversity. The diversity we want must be intentionally pursued, but cannot be manufactured.

The Church is diverse by nature of Jesus' invitation to follow Him, not by an organizational decree. Forced diversity is not beneficial because the mere existence of diversity does not necessarily produce the results we want. It is *how* the individuals relate to one another within the collective that makes the difference.

For the group of Seven Influential Neighbors to be most effective, the next starting point establishes how the individuals within the group must engage within a roundtable culture.

IT'S A ROUNDTABLE, NOT A BOARDROOM

In a boardroom, there is hierarchy and often limited ownership. Only shareholders own a piece of the company, and the CEO or chairman makes the executive decisions. The focus is execution and strategy. In a roundtable culture, however, everyone is an owner and all titles, positions of power, and influences outside the group are checked at the door. And the first priority here must be on relationships. Though strategy is important, relationships are the bedrock upon which strategies must be built. Without relationships, the key element of trust that causes collective strategies to succeed is lost.

Within a hierarchy structure, the result is *discussion*. This is the sort of group conversation where individuals make their points and "win" an argument. With discussion, there are winners and losers. It is a debate where emotions are closely tied to the individual's point of view.

Within the Seven Influential Neighbors, however, the goal is learning, not winning. By facilitating a roundtable environment, it sets the stage for controlled *dialogue*. This is the sort of group conversation where individuals are able to suspend their own ideas and perspectives to allow others to give feedback into their presuppositions. From the Greek *"dia"* meaning "through" and *"logos"* meaning words. It is "through words" that we can share ideas and come together. This is a group dynamic where ideas do not define identity and learning can occur through a genuine openness to hear what others bring to the table. In *discussion* one sub-group or individual wins, but in *dialogue* everyone wins.

Roundtable environments don't mean there won't be sparks! This is what I imagine Solomon meant when he wrote, "As iron sharpens iron, so one person sharpens another" (Proverbs 27:17 NIV). Genuine relationships between diverse individuals challenge and stretch us beyond our comfort zones. It is okay to engage with energy and passion as long as we remember that how we engage does matter. We can disagree without being disagreeable. Establishing this culture needs to be specifically addressed openly with the group. Then it needs to be readdressed, because our norm is to revert to the top-down hierarchical environments we typically operate in.

I remember being in a meeting a few years ago when our Gathering Place team was planning an outreach event for our area. We were a wonderfully diverse and passionate group of people, which allowed for quite a few sparks! I always attempted to guide the conversation into *dialogue* (although things can bleed into *discussion* quickly). This particular meeting, we were evaluating the various venues and locations for the event, and the team was going back and forth weighing the options. Two staff members in particular could not seem to understand why each other was so fixated on their preferred venue option. One was more in tune with the at-risk population in our community, and the other was more in tune with the middle-class and affluent population. They were struggling to articulate why they believed their option was the best, but after dialogue, the learning that occurred for both was awesome to watch. For one, the major issue was transportation to the venue. From his understanding of the community, it had to be a location that people could get to easily. For the other, the major issue was the safety of the venue. It had to be a place people perceived to be safe. As they learned from each other about the diversity of needs and perspectives, the end result was choosing a venue that met the needs of the *largest* number of people in the community. Our event was much more successful because our team was committed to staying at the table in an environment where diverse relationships were the foundation upon which the strategies were designed.

STAY AT THE TABLE

This last starting point is probably the hardest. Initiating diverse relationships is relatively easy compared with staying committed after the launch energy fades or when others let you down. The long haul takes some grit with a deep understanding of why unity matters so much to God. Our pledge must be to fight for relationships with other believers no matter what may come. **This is the key: commit, right from the beginning, that your relationships are never on the negotiating table.**

Starting is easier than maintaining when it comes to relationships. None of us is perfect, so when we disappoint one another we cannot give up. In fact, this is when we need to press in. We cannot force other people to stay at the table, and that's not our responsibility. If we quit on relationships when it gets hard, the enemy wins.

> Commit, right from the beginning, that your relationships are never on the negotiating table.

We have many spiritual siblings who are on different growth levels. The Bible talks about growing from baby to child to son—so there is a growing-up process in the life of the believer. When we become a son or daughter, we also enter into new relationships with other spiritual siblings who will be on different growth trajectories. This perspective is important because it gives us the ability to extend grace to those around us. As a father, I want my children to love each other, prefer each other, and be united, but I know it is a process.

This same process is at the heart of the Christian experience. Our covenant family demands allegiance to our brothers and sisters in Christ over and above any worldly allegiance. The Gospel message does not elevate the individual, as proclaimed by Western capitalism, nor does it lower the status of the individual for the greater whole, as proclaimed by socialism. God's kingdom is the only place where each person has both individual significance and greater purpose through one collective body. Therefore, we have a responsibility to stay committed to each other because we all are of value.

It is time that we resolve to stop sitting on our hands and begin to employ the leverage Christ has given us in our relationships! Authentic relationships are a powerful weapon against the spirits of competition and individualism that plague us. When we stay at the table, we communicate the power of God's grace in our faith community.

This commitment to stay at the table doesn't only declare God's grace, but also becomes a massive trust builder. If distrust is the great silent killer of unity, then trust is the great fuel. This is why leadership guru Patrick Lencioni points out that the absence of trust is the foundational dysfunction of a team or organization.[9] We tend to have a natural mistrust of things we don't know. It's a natural self-preservation tactic to avoid costly or painful surprises. The unknown makes us skeptical, and that is precisely why staying at the table is so important. In the context of relationships, the unknown becomes known.

MIKE'S STORY

One of the last things we all need is another meeting, but I am convinced that some meetings we just flat out leave too soon. It takes time to build relationships. It takes time to trust each other with our stories. It takes time to effectively share our resources. And it definitely takes time to find out where God is working, and join Him.

What is God saying to us about our relationship with Him and the caring of our souls? What is God saying to us about how we reach our community and serve the needs of those around us? Our nature is to be in a hurry to *do* for Jesus rather than to *be* for Jesus.

> What I mean is this: we are often in a hurry to plan the next event or good idea when the real challenge is to first know each other and come together to plan a "God idea." Often we delegate just enough of the idea to create an event that then has minimal impact.
>
> It takes time to prayerfully plan and develop God ideas. Let's be still, stay at the table, and see what He really wants us to join Him in doing to make a difference in our cities.

We must note here that your Seven Influential Neighbors are not designed to be a new clique or a permanent small group community. Consider that for the starlings, their Seven Influential Neighbors are in flux and motion. These relationships are designed to teach us, to give us the ability to *anticipate* the movements of other believers, and to build the vital *trust* we need. You may find yourself in and out of relationships with other believers in different seasons for different purposes. Don't hinder the possibilities by taking an overly structured approach to unity. This is not intended to be a new "in-group" that becomes exclusive. For you, your Seven Influential Neighbors might be individuals that change from time to time, depending on the projects God has you working on. Experiment with it, invite, learn, contribute, and go with the flow of the waves in the Murmurations!

Though individual experiences may differ, churches and ministries that have taken such a step to build relationships have found this truth: when believers, churches, and ministries lay hold of their interconnectedness within the Body of Christ,

God's impact through them becomes limitless! Each and every step we endeavor to take toward unity delights the Lord, but we can take those steps only when we stay at the table.

> When believers, churches, and ministries lay hold of their interconnectedness within the Body of Christ, God's impact through them becomes limitless!

A GUIDING DIAGRAM

But what is all this relationship building for?

Strategy. God wants to use our relationships to execute his strategy in the world and unleash his Kingdom through the Church. The relationships with our Seven Influential Neighbors create trust, anticipation, and efficiency for the greater purpose of developing high leverage strategies for our communities.

Through our relationships, we not only become the answer to Jesus' prayer for unity in John 17, we also become the answer to His prayer in Matthew 6 that God's Kingdom come on earth just as it is in heaven. This is not just because we "look like heaven" in our diversity, but because when kingdom-minded believers build relationships, outreach strategies will naturally emerge.

Successful movements toward unity are all founded on two key pillars: **relationships** *and* **strategy**. Both are critical.

In the next chapter, we will explore the starlings' common strategy through the Murmuration, but before we do, we need to establish a guiding diagram for our movement that builds a bridge between the two cornerstone elements of relationships and strategy.

Consider this guiding diagram:

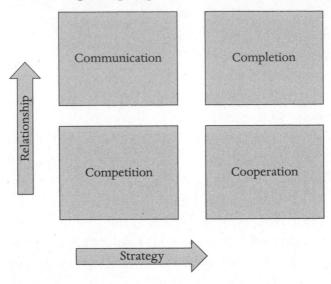

Completion matrix (Lucas Ramirez)

There are four main quadrants in this diagram from the *Harvard Business Review*:[10] in the bottom left is *competition*, above that in the upper left is the *communication* block, in the bottom right is *cooperation*, and in the upper right-hand quadrant is *completion*. The other two key elements of this diagram are the X and Y axis. The horizontal X axis represents growing strategy, and the vertical Y axis represents growing relationships.

This is an extremely helpful tool to analyze a baseline for our unity with other believers, churches, or ministries. Whether we know it or not, every individual, family, company, church, or organization is somewhere on this matrix—directly in the middle of a quadrant or in transition between quadrants.

The good news and bad news is that we can move around and between each block or quadrant. We can move up or down, forward or backward.

This diagram has been one of my guiding tools for over a decade, but the day I overlaid this diagram on top of the Murmuration principles, I was blown away. The starlings live this diagram. They engage in relationships and common strategy so seamlessly, they explode into the most desirable quadrant for any group: the *completion* block. How amazing it was to see that our best management and leadership research is merely an echo of God's beautiful design all around us.

As the diagram shows, the key elements that drive where we fall on the matrix are relationships and strategy.

Competition Block

The bottom left is a place of absolute competition with others. There is no relationship or strategy in this segment. It is the worst place to be, and the enemy's strategy is to keep us there!

Communication Block

Now, if relationships begin to develop and grow, we move vertically away from the *competition* quadrant to the *communication* block. This is a healthy advance that happens when we develop solid relationships with those around us (including our Seven Influential Neighbors). Relationships move us away from *competition* into the *communication* space because anticipation allows us to avoid crashing or inadvertently competing with others. The truth is, when we spend time with each other, we communicate freely. Deep conversations do not happen on social media, and wrestling with truth through character limits is almost impossible. A friendship, however, provides the opportunity for shared experiences, ideas, information, and diverse perspectives.

Cooperation Block

Starting again in the *competition* quadrant, we move horizontally into the *cooperation* block if there is a common strategy. When a unified strategy exists, like cleaning up a community after a flood, the benefit of cooperating together toward a common goal becomes very clear. With a shared strategy, cooperation promotes the sharing of resources to help one another reach a common goal. Without relationship in the mix, however, cooperation is usually strictly driven by mutual goals.

This produces positive outcomes because things "get done" in this space. **But the vision for the Murmuration movement is much deeper than only** *communication* **or** *collaboration*. **Many times, we have mistakenly settled for either communication or collaboration, thinking that we have unity.** Jesus did not pray for His followers to just work together or simply be in relationship, He prayed that His followers would be *one as the Trinity is one.*

Some of us are experts at fellowship, worship, prayer, or teaching. Others can execute incredible programs and collaborate around a conference or special outreach event. However, we tend to stay in either the competition, communication, or collaboration blocks. What we miss is that we were designed for more than simply living in these blocks. We have an incredible opportunity to enter into a whole new sphere. When both *relationships and strategy* grow simultaneously, we move into the sweet spot for our oneness: the *completion block.*

Completion Block

This is where the power of unity lies.

Our goal must be the fourth quadrant: *completion.* The only way that we can reach this allusive quadrant is when both relationships and common strategy grow simultaneously. This is *Murmuration* territory. This is the unity Christ prayed for!

Completion is also the quadrant Paul calls the Church to be in:

> For just as the body is one and has many members, and all the members of the body, though many, are one body, so it is with Christ...For the body does not consist of one member but of many...The eye cannot say to the hand, "I have no need of you," nor again the head to the feet, "I have no need of you."...Now you are the body of Christ and individually members of it.
>
> 1 Corinthians 12:12, 14, 21, 27 ESV

Operating in this space causes a sense of belonging to a team where everyone understands their role and purpose in the body. The *completion* space is what we must all work toward for our organizations, our families, our communities, and the Church!

Can you imagine? What if churches and ministries had growing relationships, communicated clearly, and their authentic sharing of resources accomplished common goals and strategies for their city? They would be an unstoppable force. And it's exactly what God has in mind for His Church.

As we mature away from division and become a murmurating church, our completion will look more like this:

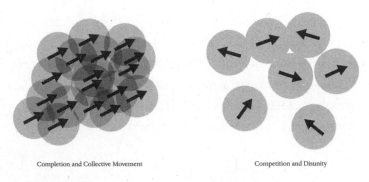

Completion and Collective Movement   Competition and Disunity

Completion and collective movement (Lucas Ramirez)

In the echo chambers of our silos, we look like the image on the right, each moving and working in a direction we hope is best. Either unaware or indifferent, we ultimately lose our power. With relationships and common strategy, we can look more like the image on the left: a complete body with power, focus, and concentrated energy.

You might be wondering, if there are so many people and ministries in the world, isn't there a natural limit to how many relationships we can have? The Murmuration has a roadmap for us here too. Research shows that the starlings actually understand their role in a larger system through their relationship with those immediately around them. It is the *local* interactions that make them aware of the *global* movements of the entire flock.[11] We don't need direct contact and relationship with everyone. If we keep the right number of micro relationships, we will have a pulse on the macro interactions.

We don't have to know everyone, but the first step is to know someone. Identify your influencing neighbors and let relationship and strategy increase at the individual and organizational levels. The bottom line is that if we are ever to reach the *completion* sphere, relationship and strategy are inseparable. The starlings know who they are, who they fly with, and the strategy behind why they murmurate.

It is time we take notes from the starlings.

Chapter 5

Principle 2: Collective Strategy— Focus on the Common Enemy

When God sets out to embrace the enemy, the result is the cross.

—Miroslav Volf[1]

Beholding the beautiful swooping and majestic aerial twisting of a Murmuration causes us to wonder at not only the mechanics of *how*, but also the *why*.

Why do starlings murmurate?

For years, scientist and nature enthusiasts have wanted to know the driving purpose behind Murmurations. Some hypothesized it was related to gathering warmth, which may be a helpful by-product, but recent science has revealed that starlings murmurate because of a shared collective strategy: defend against the attack of a common enemy. In this new research, done with data from over three thousand Murmurations, scientists found that "the collective behavior observed in starling Murmurations is primarily an anti-predator adaptation."[2]

Rather than trying to devise their own individual survival plans, they are intensely committed to one another through a collective strategy. And they are fully committed to the bigger picture, knowing that when the flock wins, they all win.

Alone, they don't stand a chance against their deadly predators such as buzzards and hawks. But in numbers, they have power—even more power when the mass can operate as one super organism. As they leverage the power of relationships, they execute the same goal, and the Murmuration becomes a garrison for their flock—relationships and strategy in rhythm.

Social learning is a major value for many birds, mostly when it comes to learning to recognize predators or threats. Although some responses to predators are hard-wired, other birds learn about dangers by watching older birds.[3] For the starlings, they can actually learn how to visually distinguish between their predators and other birds of similar species that look like their predators.[4] We know this because only the birds of prey, and not crows or gulls, have a direct impact on the size and duration of the Murmurations even though gulls and crows resemble the real predators closely. Starlings are intensely vigilant to spot their *true* enemies.

One of the starling's main predators is the peregrine falcon. Like the top gun fighter jet of nature, the peregrine is one of the world's fiercest predators. Falcons fly high above their prey and perform incredible nosedives to attack from overhead. In these dives, the falcon has the ability to reach speeds up to two hundred miles per hour, literally making it the fastest animal on the planet in those moments. If it were not for the falcon's special nostrils, the air pressure alone would crush its lungs. This amazing feature is so advanced, it is used in jet engines today!

How do you defend against one of the most elite predators in the world?

You murmurate.

And get ready for this: the more fierce the attack, the more beautiful the formation becomes.

Falcons skirt around the edge of the flock, but they will not dare dive straight into the thick density of a Murmuration. **The most effective defense against the most elite predator is unity.**

> The more fierce the attack, the more beautiful the formation becomes.

A COMMON ENEMY

Followers of Christ have an elite and ruthlessly deadly predator too. Scripture calls us to be sober-minded and watchful because "your adversary the devil prowls around like a roaring lion, seeking someone to devour" (1 Peter 5:8 ESV). As believers, we have protection in the Holy Spirit, but the 1 Peter warning was directed at Christians. There is still a predator on the loose with velociraptor instincts—the most manipulative and merciless predator you can imagine. In our comfortable environments, we sometimes forget we are up against a very real and direct threat. Every moment, the enemy fills his time seeking what he can steal and kill and destroy (John 10:10 ESV). It is no wonder that in Jesus' prayer for unity in John 17, He correlates our unity directly with our protection. Jesus knew exactly what we would be up against. This is why He prayed:

*Holy Father, **protect them by the power of your name, the name
you gave me, so that they may be one as we are one** ... My
prayer is not that you take them out of the world but that you
protect them from the evil one.*

John 17:11, 15 NIV, emphasis added

The problem is that in large part, we have embarrassingly
identified the wrong enemy—we have made our neighbors
our foe. How can we ever possibly develop collective strategy
to defend against an enemy that we can't all agree upon? No
doubt this is also a deception of the true enemy.

With no clear collective strategy for either defense or
offense, we have fallen into his trap and find ourselves divided
and confused on the battlefield. We are exposed and playing
defense against all sorts of different "enemies." Sometimes
even over mere personal preference, we have turned on one
another, seeing fellow brothers and sisters in Christ as enemies. All the while the true enemy sits back and laughs. He
doesn't even have to show up to the battle if he can keep us
fighting each other.

In the Greek language, the word *diabolos* for devil basically means "scatterer," someone who throws things apart.[5]
Or consider the word "sin," derived from the German *sunde*,
which carries connotations of sundering or dividing. From
the very beginning, the enemy's strategy has been to divide
and cause radical schisms between man, God, and all created
things.

Remember Paul's emphasis on unity in his letter to the
Ephesians:

He made known to us the mystery of His will...that
is, the summing up of all things in Christ, things in the
heavens and things on the earth.

Ephesians 1:9–10 NASB

The devil is the divider, but Christ is the great unifier. Or
you could put it like this: if God's strategy is unity, then Satan's
mission is division. We must elevate the priority of unity in
our faith community and realize that when we see our fellow
believers as the enemy, we weaken the Gospel and strengthen
the enemy's strategy. **The first step in moving toward unity
despite our differences is identifying the *correct* common
enemy.** And nothing unites people like a common enemy.

MIKE'S STORY

A few years back, a group of national leaders were meeting in D.C. They were there to dream about how they could
continue to work together to reach the next generation for
Christ. In the midst of their meetings, they had the unique
opportunity to visit the pentagon and meet with one of the
joint chiefs at the time, Admiral Clark. In the interest of networking, the group asked the admiral, "How is it that you
get along here with the different military organizations?"
Without hesitation, the admiral responded: "It's one word:
'war.' In peace time we have a tendency to get distracted,
but in the midst of a war, we have to work together."

We have to redefine who our real enemy is through deep introspection, even repentance for treating our brother as an enemy. In relationships, our differences dissipate almost instantly when we refocus our energy on our true adversary, the divider. Today, the enemy's strategy remains the same, and wherever backbiting, mutual hatred, isolation, unrest, or unresolved conflict exists, our adversary the devil and the sin in our hearts are at work.

The starlings in a Murmuration never collide because they all have the same strategy built on relationships and awareness. It's crystal clear in their minds who the *real* enemy is. For the Church, we are confused about which direction to fly in and which enemy to flee from, leaving us incapable of murmurating.

MIKE'S STORY

One of the most significant experiences of common strategy I've ever been a part of in twenty years of bringing people together started in 2016. It began with conversations at a Mission America event in Long Beach, California, where leaders from all sectors were present to strategize kingdom-building efforts. Mission America networks leaders from churches, denominations, ministries, networks, and city movements, calling the whole Church to take the whole Gospel to the whole Nation—and to the world.

For us, it was a time to get to know one another, sharing our stories and bringing our strengths to the table. Enough happened in the meetings that year for us to realize the conversation wasn't over.

Chuck Klein from Campus Alliance and I started to meet afterward to dream about what could happen if organizations and ministries gathered around the same passion of reaching students with the Gospel and brought their best to the table. Our approach and strategies may be different but together, could we see *every* student and *every* school reached?

That's the passion that birthed a collective of leaders in Southern California called ESES: Every School, Every Student. Three months later, Biola University hosted our first gathering for key leaders to come to the table and develop a common strategy. Quickly, our fellowship continued to grow and now we have fifty leaders in Southern California committed from local churches and para-church ministries like Youth for Christ, Fellowship of Christian Athletes, CRU, Moms in Prayer, Christian Educators, Gateways to Better Education, and Young Life. *Many had never even met one another before and didn't realize the resource they could be for one another.*

The *Every Student and Every School Forum* now convenes two times a year, with many individual conversations taking place between meetings. One time I gave a leader twenty dollars and challenged him to meet with another leader in between meetings. It warmed my heart when I got a text with a picture of them having lunch together. It's amazing what can happen when people come to the table and stay at the table to develop common strategies.

It's been so much fun to hear the stories of how the leaders are connecting and supporting one another. We have each other's backs and make each other better! The common strategy for reaching every student shows the power of relationship and common strategy at work.

This is the result of *years* of tilling the ground for unity. This is the fruit of working together and laying this foundation when hardly anyone was showing up. But we kept going, committed to relationships and common strategy. As my ninth-grade history teacher would say, the roots of the present are deep in the past.

OUR NEIGHBORS ARE NEVER OUR ENEMY

Focusing on the correct enemy day after day can be difficult. It is a discipline to learn, because it is so easy to focus on our competition, who is visible, instead of our enemy, who is invisible. Like the starlings, it is critical to identify the true predator and remember that there is no *one* to blame about our current divided state. It is not *their* fault. We all carry some responsibility because we are a system—a body that moves forward or backward together.

In his letter to the Galatians, Paul admonishes the early church that "The entire law is fulfilled in keeping this one command: 'Love your neighbor as yourself.' If you bite and devour

each other, watch out or you will be destroyed by each other"
(Galatians 5:14–15 NIV). And just a few verses later he delivers
the beautiful list of the fruits of the Spirit. Now, I invite you to
re-read Galatians 5 with Ephesians 1 in the backdrop (that the
summing up of God's will was to bring everything together in
unity through Christ):

> But the fruit of the Spirit is love, joy, peace, forbear-
> ance, kindness, goodness, faithfulness, gentleness and
> self-control. Against such things there is no law. Those
> who belong to Christ Jesus have crucified the flesh with
> its passions and desires. Since we live by the Spirit, let us
> keep in step with the Spirit. Let us not become conceited,
> provoking and envying each other.
>
> Galatians 5:22–26 NIV

This Galatians passage carries so much more significance
through the lens of unity in the Body. It is not just about living the fruits of the Spirit for ourselves or family, but bearing
these fruits is the road map for walking into unity and loving
our neighbors. Maybe you think your church or ministry is
the best (*conceited* v. 26) or you think you're the worst (*envy-
ing* v. 26). Or maybe you're somewhere in the middle just
stirring the pot (*provoking* v. 26). Wherever you are, we echo
Christ's words and invite you to respond to Jesus' command to
love your neighbors as yourselves. When we love our neighbors instead of making them our enemies, they become our
allies for building the Kingdom. This is the dance, rhythm,
and power of combining growing relationship with collective
strategy!

Real change will come when we take the first step of changing the way we think. This *metanoia*—a change of thinking that impacts the way we live—will ripple powerfully through the Church. It will provide a new conceptual framework to define the social and physical structures we create. A redeemed way of thinking will elevate the importance of relationships and strategy to move us away from *competition* and toward *completion*.

We envision entire staff or volunteer departments being developed for this work of unity. Wouldn't it be revolutionary to actually strengthen some of our job descriptions by adding the responsibility for being the connection point with our Seven Influential Neighbors and other ministries? This new way of thinking will allow us to be the Church that creates the future—God's future—rather than simply reacting to events that happen.

None of this, however, comes free.[6] Relationships are an investment of time, and common strategies will require shared resources. But it is worth it. May our formations become increasingly more beautiful even in the midst of fierce attacks from the enemy. In the context of relationships, may our common strategy and focus on the true enemy give us the advantage as we defend effectively and develop *offensive* strategies for our communities.

Chapter 6

Principle 3: Critical Mass

As long as individual Christians journey alone—no matter how "radical" they are—their effect will be minimal.

—David Platt[1]

The Murmuration phenomenon is so awe-inspiring that scientists compare it more to transition physics than biology. Think in terms of metal becoming magnetized or water becoming a vapor. Murmurations are critical systems that are on the brink. Part starling, part flock, part movement. Fully Murmuration. It is an amazing system that is already but not yet fully what it can become.

To think in terms of transition physics rather than biology, we need to know three important terms: Phase. Phase boundary. Critical point.

Stay with me. This is incredible.

All material or matter is categorized in **phases**: solid, liquid, gas, and so on. The "phase" a material is in represents the external conditions (temperature or pressure) that allow that material to be uniform. But if you change the external factors, such as increase the temperature, you disrupt the equilibrium and push materials to their **phase boundary**, the point at which a material changes between phases. Whenever you've boiled water, you have seen thermodynamics and phase transitions at work.

Okay, here is the amazing part.

If just the right combination of a specific temperature and pressure exist, then materials can hit what is called the **critical point**. This is an amazing zone where phase boundaries vanish and two phases of the same material can actually **coexist**.[2] With water, for example, the critical point is the only time that the substance can be liquid and have *the same* density, pressure, and temperature as the same substance that is in the gas phase.[3] Basically, it means that at the critical point, water can be either liquid or gas at the same time. Individual starling and flock at the same time. Flock and Murmuration at the same time.

As research from Cavagna and others shows, with the right circumstances, one of the unbelievable qualities of the Murmuration is its state of criticality; the flock is poised and continuously ready to tip into a Murmuration phase.

That is why it would not be accurate to merely call it a "flock" of starlings in the same way that it would not be correct to call a liquid a vapor. The word "flock" wouldn't capture the true essence of the phenomena. Just like water and vapor can coexist at the critical point, in the Murmuration, the individual and the collective coexist.

Criticality also means that in the Murmuration **a new entity actually emerges within the group** when the birds come together in their special way. They were designed for a third "phase" where the group becomes *more* than the sum of its parts.[4] It is no longer just the individual birds or a flock of birds; they become a super organism that moves as one because they *are* one.

THE NEED FOR CRITICAL MASS TO REACH THE CRITICAL POINT

If temperature and pressure are the things that get water to the critical point, what then are the factors that get a flock of starlings to the "critical" point? How do they transition from being simply a gathering of birds into something with collective order and cohesive movement?

There is still much speculation among scientists regarding all the elements that get a starling flock to a critical point. Some factors actually include temperature, external noise, and pressure from a predator. Other experts postulate that reaching criticality is possible not only through external forces, but also through hard-wired instinctual behavior.[5]

Although there is still mystery around all the exact factors and environment needed for starlings to transition into a Murmuration, we do know there is one vital factor that must be present: **density of the flock**.[6] You can't very well murmurate with ten birds. To hit the critical point, the starlings need a critical mass.

Scientists have not standardized the exact threshold of birds or the critical mass needed for a Murmuration, but combining the baseline data from various groups of researchers gives us a solid range of an estimated minimum of four hundred to five hundred starlings.[7,8,9] This means that a critical mass of four hundred to five hundred starlings is absolutely required before the Murmuration can come to life. Can you begin to see the beautiful implications?

IT'S GOT TO BE CRITICAL

Unity has to be *critical* to enough people, so that through our *critical mass* we can reach the *critical point* of unleashing a new *phase* of the Church. This might be something the world has never seen.

Just like the Murmurations, the Christian Church needs a critical mass of people wholly committed to Christ's vision for unity. This is absolutely essential if we have any hopes of getting to what Gladwell calls the *tipping point*—"the moment of critical mass, the threshold, the boiling point."[10] For the Church, the tipping point will be when a critical mass of Christians across the world know that the mission of God rests in our ability to operate as one body.

This means that if God is lighting a fire in you right now through this message, then you must share it. If Christ is opening your eyes to see the great heights we were designed for, then you have to help us hit a critical mass! Our greatest potential lies in unified kingdom strategies, and it is *your* responsibility to share this message. Share this book, post messages and Scriptures that point us to oneness, find ways in conversation to bring up God's great passion for unity. Our faith communities are so dehydrated and devoid of this message that it will require everyday leaders like us to bring this conversation to the forefront. God is inviting you into the fellowship so that you can turn around and invite others.

Our movement is density dependent. If the Church has any hopes to move as one, and transition from our state of division to an entirely new way of operating, it will require us coming together to reach a critical point. We won't know the magic number, but we will know it when we reach it. When we do, all of a sudden, a collective unified movement will emerge as the Church experiences a phase transition. Right before our very eyes, the Holy Spirit will conduct the Church while we play effortless acrobatics and reach our highest potential to love, serve, and heal the world. It will be like being in "the wave" in a stadium. We will not really know who started it, but suddenly, it will be upon us, and we will be in it, responding appropriately to the movements of other believers around us.

THE CRITICAL MASS BEHIND THE IPHONE

June 29, 2007, was a historic day. People waited in line for hours for the release of the very first iPhone. And when over 250,000 phones sold in the first two days, Apple secured its position as an iconic, culture-shaping company. From the iPod to the iPhone and iPad, the company has changed communications and the way we consume digital media. Then, roughly one year later in July 2008, Apple opened the App Store—a virtual store for software that makes your phone more productive to meet the needs of your lifestyle. Within the first month, the App Store generated $1 million a day in sales and by 2010, there were over 250,000 apps available for users. Now, there are over two million apps.

The App Store is probably one of the most overlooked innovations that drive the success of Apple. We take for granted this modern-day marvel, yet it is one of the most fascinating examples of the power of critical mass. Apple knew that a single company could never produce the innovation, creativity, and sheer volume of applications that the App Store would demand. They needed developers. A lot of them. So they opened up profit sharing and created a marketplace for developers and consumers. By doing this, Apple quickly recruited the critical mass of developers that they needed. As of this writing, Apple boasts 180 billion app downloads with $70 billion paid out to developers.

Imagine if the App Store had never reached the critical mass of developers it needed. It would not be a very exciting place with only a handful of apps. Apple designed it to be an incredible community of productivity, but it needed a critical mass of people to buy into the vision and they needed to look beyond their own internal Apple team. Without that, it would have never reached the full potential it was designed for.

In the Church, God has designed us for so much more. When He imagined the Church, He saw diverse tribes, languages, genders, and cultures also forming a beautiful community of productivity. He set the environment for us to live daringly different lives from the world around us. Loving one another in spite of our differences. Forgiving one another in spite of past hurts. The Church is designed to soar, but we will never attain our fullest potential without the critical mass we need.

It is up to *me* and *you* to begin living it and inviting others into the vision, lest we hear the haunting words of Christ, "Why do you call me 'Lord, Lord,' and do not do what I say?" (Luke 6:46 NIV). We must put away pride from our hearts. Stomp out narcissism from our minds. Uproot unforgiveness and eradicate individualism and competition. Ground zero is in our own hearts first.

Unfortunately, today the critical mass of believers is trending toward disunity. It is time to grow the numbers of those who buy into the unity vision by sharing ideas through whatever platform God has blessed you with. Let's reach the point of critical mass and see, maybe for the first time, the Church transition into a phase the likes of which we have never seen.

I love this idea of critical mass because it perfectly balances the importance of the individual *and* the whole. It emphasizes again the great value of the entire Christian community. We can have all the ideas, solutions, and strategies in the world, but if enough individuals do not catch the vision to build the kingdom together, the gears of the movement will remain gridlocked. We can have all the hope and faith, too, but without enough people, we will not hit the critical mass to murmurate in our communities. We absolutely need each other.

Chapter 7

Principle 4: Recognition of Mutual Need

The eye cannot say to the hand, "I don't need you!" And the head cannot say to the feet, "I don't need you!"

— 1 Corinthians 12:21 NIV

The transfer of information is one of the most important things in our world. Without the right information, things go sideways fast. We miss appointments, we can't make wise decisions or operate at our fullest capacity. Google and other tech giants have made a business out of gathering, sharing, storing, and selling information. Information can be hard to get, difficult to keep, and even more difficult to pass along accurately and efficiently. Even with our sophisticated communication systems, we don't always get the memo. We misread a text, overlook an email, a signal can be weak, or data files get corrupted.

Think back to the games Telephone or Whisper Down the Lane where a phrase is passed from person to person in hopes of keeping the integrity of the original phrase until the end of the line. Most of the time, you'd be lucky to get the same phrase at the end with just five players. It's common logic: the larger a business, school, hospital, army, or any group of people is, the harder the sharing of accurate information will become.

But not so in a Murmuration. Check this out.

An Italian research team showed that the sharing of information between starlings in a Murmuration is almost "not decaying with distance."[1] Of all the beautiful and fascinating things that surfaced while studying Murmurations, by far the most exotic feature was this *scale-free correlation*. At its core, it is the idea that a Murmuration can continue to scale, and regardless of how big it gets, the phenomena *will still continue to work*. Let me explain.

When a bird on the outer part of the flock banks inward toward the formation, this information gets distributed almost instantaneously throughout the entire flock—regardless of how far the information needs to travel. The same research group also found that "the effective perception range of each individual is as large as the entire group and it becomes possible to transfer undamped information to all animals, no matter their distance, making the group respond as one."[2]

In other words *it doesn't matter how large the flock becomes, collective movement will still occur and the starlings' ability to share information will scale as the flock grows*. Size truly doesn't matter. The starlings' core behavioral rules allow for the Murmuration to work whether the flock has five hundred birds or one hundred thousand birds. Exactly how the birds keep such strong transfer of information across space and a huge mass of birds is still a mystery to scientists.

The scale-free nature of Murmurations provides the birds with **the ability to perceive connections within the larger flock**. Although "no individual knows the size or shape of the flock,"[3] the local interactions between a starling and its seven neighbors connects them to the global flock. Research goes on to say that "the behavioral change of one individual influences and is influenced by the behavioral change of all other individuals in the group."[4] In a Murmuration, we not only witness the emergence of global order from local interactions, but the science also shows that the birds actually perceive they are part of something greater than themselves.

The results are nearly mystical. A single starling affects the larger group and the group formation simultaneously affects the single starling. This shows that the phenomena is not just a reflex, rather an intentional coming together. They realize how much they need one another. The birds recognize the mutual need they have for one another and see that they need one other to accomplish the greater strategy.

Let your imagination run wild for a minute—what if God designed the Church for scale-free correlation too? What if scale-free correlation was the same power that God had in mind when He designed the Church to be one body? He knew how large, diverse, and geographically scattered His people would be one day, and yet, empowered by the Holy Spirit, would have the potential for a scale-free correlation of our own.

Before we can move toward this collective movement, we must first realize deep in our gut just how much we need one another. We must be convinced that we will never accomplish alone the things we were designed to do together.

REWIND

Rewind to 2006—it's 3:00 p.m. on a hot Sunday afternoon in coastal Georgia. I am the rookie youth pastor at a large local church. I arrive at church two hours early to set up for our Sunday night program, but quickly become overwhelmed as I review the length of my to-do list. There's just no way to accomplish everything before my students arrive at 5:00 p.m.

There's the music to organize and song sheets to photocopy. *Where did I last see that projector? Oh, yeah, the pastor's office—all the way on the opposite side of the building!*

The chairs in the youth room, scattered like a deck of cards, are in need of arranging. Day after day, I kick dodge balls out of my path. Why is it so hard to find one now? With keyboards, music stands, extra chairs, and an LCD projector in tow (as well as a cow's tongue for a crazy teaching illustration), I find myself sprinting through a labyrinth of church hallways. Setup for youth-group gatherings requires herculean multi-tasking.

Feeling alone, I begin to realize that some of my stress is self-inflicted. Being responsible for so many different tasks, I feel more like a prizefighter in the ring, focused on the many rounds with my opponent before me:

Round 1: Ice-breaker—lead an exciting and engaging game that no student can resist.

Round 2: Lead worship in a way that rocks out, but brings students to their knees as they focus on Jesus.

Round 3: In general, just be awesome all of the time to keep the students focused and engaged and to keep any volunteers feeling useful and valued.

Round 4: Share a meaningful, memorable, and relevant teaching.

Round 5: Lead small group discussions that help students apply God's truth to their lives.

Round 6: Stay late with a kid(s) whose parents forgot to pick him up and/or with the kid(s) who need help as they wrestle with what's troubling them.

Round 7: Clean up. Tomorrow is another day in the life of this busy church and the staff expect to find everything pristine and in its proper place in the morning.

With so many rounds, and not always a lot of visible rewards, I feel exhausted and discouraged. Who wouldn't?

Your journey, context, or job might be different, but if you've ever felt **alone**, it can be totally overwhelming. I remember finishing up late one night with my back literally against the wall outside the youth gathering room. I slid down the wall to a sitting position and thought: *It's just not possible to do ministry alone.* I felt isolated and knew I was missing something. This was a critical moment for me. I was on the knife's edge of seeing, possibly for the first time, the theme of unity God had weaved into my life.

THE COFFEE SHOP

We all know how crucial a volunteer team is for ministry, but since I didn't have one of those handy, I turned to a new friend and fellow youth pastor in the area, David. After attending a conference together, we decided to meet once a week at a local coffee shop. We prayed for each other and shared ideas about ministry, family, and work. Over time, our relationship organically grew into a strategy that God faithfully sparked for our groups to come together for a special event in unity. Jesus' prayer was a launching pad:

> The goal is for all of them to become one heart and mind—just as you, Father, are in me and I in you, so they might be one heart and mind with us. Then the world might believe that you, in fact, sent me. The same glory you gave me, I gave them, so they'll be as unified and together as we are—I in them and you in me. Then they'll be mature in this oneness.
>
> John 17:21–23b MSG

We decided to walk into this vision and give it a shot as best we knew how. We would plan and host an event together—joining our youth groups and churches for one night. We called it Fusion.

THE EVENT

We let our creative juices flow and organized an event that surpassed what any of us could have accomplished separately.

Rather than spreading ourselves too thin, and going all seven rounds on our own, we shared all the responsibilities of the event. Collaborating allowed us to concentrate on completing our necessary tasks and do each one well. It was a lighter workload, a shared financial burden, and turned out to be a much better program. The Lord had creatively resolved our problem and simultaneously created a springboard from His greater purposes! We did not discover a new program, rather God revealed to us how to proceed in His Church. They were basic and simple steps, but we were walking in the right direction. *We didn't realize the fullness of what God was doing among us until after we followed the vision He gave to us.*

The first Fusion was a huge success. Students were talking, parents were talking, and soon other churches became more than curious. *What was that event you did? How did that go? When is the next one? How can we be a part of it?*

So we launched monthly Fusion events. We extended an invitation to any and all churches and youth pastors to join us, with just one condition: every church contributes. The momentum spread in our community and before long, we had six churches involved, then eight, and in rapid time, a dozen! The most amazing part of this? The churches engaged in Fusion were from a variety of denominations and traditions: Baptist, Presbyterian, Methodist, non-denominational, Roman Catholic, and Episcopal, and some with diverse cultural heritages too!

It started as a simple idea, but as it grew, Fusion communicated to our students that as followers of Christ, they belong to something bigger than themselves, even bigger than their individual home churches and denominations. We need each other.

Over the years Fusion events have changed or run their natural course. The monthly events evolved into collaborative fall and spring retreats for middle and high school students. It certainly was not always perfect, but as we began to walk into our greater design, Fusion broadcast to our entire community the reconciliation power of Christ.

KAIROS

The Greek language has two words for time: *kronos*, referring to the sequential passing of time and *kairos*, meaning a single or critical moment in time. The Fusion event was a *kairos* moment for me. It was the critical moment when I first saw the deeper themes and importance of unity in the body. That ministry experience also opened the window for me to see the beautiful theme of unity that God weaved into *kronos* and the timeline of my life. Although it took me over twenty years to see it, like blinders coming off, I finally began to see the story God was writing through my journey.

As a child, I was born in Argentina and experienced even more cultures through the international missions work of my parents. I saw also through this lens of unity within diversity through attending churches of various backgrounds and my own multi-ethnic family through the adoption of my oldest sister. Beyond that, the Lord gave me opportunities to do many collaborative international mission projects. And then came Fusion, which the Lord used to crystallize all the experiences together and ignite my passion for unity in the body of Christ. This is a central reason why I gave a hearty, "Yes" when the call to work at The Gathering Place came. It is an organization that functions so well at gathering the diverse parts of the Body of Christ, and it was clearly the next vehicle God orchestrated for me to continue working toward unity.

I saw that all along in the background, deep in my soul, a transformation of concepts and thoughts was in process. This was an unseen, long-term evolution, but it became apparent when I finally saw the tapestry coming together.

MIKE'S STORY

Has there ever been a moment in time when someone or something spoke into your life and it changed you forever? For me it was 1996. Promise Keepers was at the height of the movement and I found myself in the Georgia Dome listening to Max Lucado speak about denominational reconciliation and quoting Jesus' last prayers in John 17. Lucado's words still ring in my ears:

> Unity matters to God. Unity is a priority to God. If unity pleases God, then disunity disturbs God.
>
> Satan's master strategy is disunity. The sin of disunity has caused more souls to be lost than any other sins.

Promise Keepers propelled my passion, but my true *kairos* moment was long before that. In 1970, the Jesus Movement was exploding and our little town of Ojai, California, hosted a weeklong Billy Graham–type crusade at my local high school. The youth of our community came together in amazing ways to support the event, igniting a movement that impacted both local churches and our high school. After the crusade, students continued to gather on my campus over lunch to worship in ways we had never experienced before. We were passionate about sharing our faith with our friends, and our friends were responding openly. I felt like I was a part of one large youth group made up of various churches throughout our city (Assemblies of God, Presbyterian, Baptist, etc.). We worshipped, prayed, played, and evangelized together. Amazing. This continued for the next three or four years, but its influence on our town lasted long beyond those years.

My desire to see the Body of Christ *be better together* was birthed out of these unified relationships. Just as in Acts 17, we were experiencing God "living and moving and having His very being" within and among us, we made each other better. We brought our strengths and our passions to the table. And we witnessed an incredible openness to Jesus in people's hearts and minds, especially evident in my public high school.

Five years later, I began my first position as a full-time youth pastor at a local church in Salem, Oregon. My passion for unity continued, and I began meeting monthly with a local group of youth workers called SAYDF, Salem Area Youth Directors Fellowship. Keenly aware that we could not reach our city alone, and passionate to reach students in Salem with the good news of Jesus, we worked together. We met monthly to encourage each other, walk life together, and all the while asked ourselves, *"What can we do together that we cannot do separately?"* I loved this opportunity to be a part of something bigger than just my church.

When we found out that fifty miles north of us in Portland, youth workers from various denominations and parachurch organizations were also uniting, I began joining with them as well and we began facilitating training events for students and their leaders. It was exciting to bring our strengths to the table. We, too, were making each other better and creating opportunities to reach more students. God was doing something new in the youth ministry world and igniting a vision where our interdependence would produce impact that could have never been possible on our own

Overtime

When God called me back to California in 1986, naturally the first thing I did when moving to San Diego was to find a network of youth pastors. Out of this network I began meeting regularly with the Baptist youth pastor down the freeway. He invited me to go to Colorado to experience the Forum there, a gathering of youth leaders from around the nation facilitated by the National Network of Youth Ministries. This gathering became another milestone in my experience and call toward unity: men and women with a passion for students and a passion to be united in our effort to reach them. I was now part of a *national* movement.

I will never forget sitting at the Forum over coffee with my San Diego friend and we began to dream about doing something together in our city. His ministry had been facilitating an event called Overtime, reaching hundreds of students after football games in a "fifth quarter" event. He believed this was an event that could reach many more students if we did it together. Upon returning home we began to rally other youth leaders in our city. First problem: Where would we hold an event that would have capacity for thousands of students?

With probably some naive enthusiasm, a small group of us youth pastors "dressed up" and presented our idea to the PR people at San Diego's Sea World. Amazingly, they were excited and ready to partner with us! They had recently created a venue called "City Streets" that was highlighting BMX and skateboard riders. The timing was perfect for what we were dreaming of: a pre-evangelism event with bands, action sport guests, and a short message. We gathered for four Friday nights, concluding on the final Friday with a cheerleading contest (this was hot in the '80s!). Students were coming from all over San Diego in school-sponsored buses.

A Murmuration of our own began to form as hundreds of volunteers from various churches and para-church organizations caught the vision and joined the effort. Over a period of five years, we touched thousands of students from all over San Diego County with the message of Jesus' love in a publicly united way. But our vision began to move past collaboration and into completion only because we recognized how much we needed each other.

Twenty years later the impact of that unified strategy is still felt today by anyone involved. Incredible doors of opportunity open when someone has an idea *and doesn't care who gets the credit.*

Mike and I are not naive to think that our experiences in Georgia and California are unique to us alone. Many other leaders have shared with us their own experiences of working together and entering into deeper relationships and strategy with other ministries in their communities. God is stirring something new in His Church!

The stories vary from city to city, but regardless of where, when, or who—**these experiences have one main thing in common: they were born out of a recognition of mutual need.** They stemmed from understanding how much we truly need each other and believing we are stronger together.

This idea of deeply understanding our mutual need is the same driving force behind 1 Corinthians when Paul famously says, "The eye cannot say to the hand, 'I don't need you!' And the head cannot say to the feet, 'I don't need you!'" (1 Corinthians 12:21 NIV). The pride and arrogance of the head thinking it could stand alone without the rest of the body is almost comical. Let's get a hold of one thing:

Just as a body, though one, has many parts, but all its many parts form one body, so it is with Christ. For we were all baptized by one Spirit so as to form one body—whether Jews or Gentiles, slave or free—and we were all given the one Spirit to drink. Even so the body is not made up of one part but of many.

1 Corinthians 12:12–14 NIV

There is no misinterpreting Paul's message here. As believers, we *need* one another. But today, we have not yet truly bought into this as the global Church. Yes, we may believe we need each other within the local congregation, but that is not the whole Body of Christ.

If we have any hope of operating in the scale-free realm of power and unity God designed us for, we need new ways of thinking—individual thought-pattern changes that produce widespread results. Local interactions that produce global order. That means each of us carries a responsibility to release unity by changing the way we think. We offer two new ways of thinking to help us on our journey: new creation and systems thinking.

THE WORK OF NEW CREATION DEMANDS UNITY

So many stunning architectural elements come together to form the beautiful cathedrals of the world. In the same way, our individual persons, local congregations, and ministries are intended to complement one another and come together for a greater purpose. But this collective temple is designed by God to be a living body He indwells. His people are not meant to rest in a stationary house of worship, but rather be intensely alive, commanded to be active for the transformation and renewal of the world.

I think at times we've forgotten the profoundly missional responsibility that comes from claiming Christ as Lord. We're lulled into a sleepy state, day after day simply enjoying the American dream. It is as if we are content living safe, comfortable lives, just waiting for Christ to return or waiting until we finally pass on to heaven. **This limited view of what being a Christ follower really means has dramatically downsized the full message and power of the Gospel!** It allows us to remain comfortably divided while the world continues to hurt. Faith in Christ for too many has come to mean a religious routine or a golden ticket mentality for some post-mortem ethereal existence.

So how does this relate to unity and why is this important? **An incomplete view of the Gospel robs us of the urgency it demands.** When we understand more deeply the massive proportions of what the Gospel really calls us into, the size of our task will immediately cause us to recognize our mutual need for one another. It begins with this slight change in perspective:

Jesus didn't come just so you could go to heaven.

The individualism most dominant in the West has limited our understanding of the story of Jesus, creating a hyper focus on the individual benefits of the greater Gospel story. If the Gospel is boiled down to mean only that I get to go to heaven, the message loses so much power because there is no mission tied to the calling. Don't get me wrong, the truth that Jesus, the Son of God, willingly suffered a brutal death and vanquished sin and evil through His resurrection has direct implications and benefits for the individual. Yes, thank the Lord that as a result of Christ's work on the cross, we can have access to the Father by grace alone through faith.

But Jesus didn't *just* come so you and I could go to heaven.

He came to make *all* things new.

Consider the first part of John 3:16 (ESV): "For God so loved the world, that he gave his only Son..." We've casually interpreted this passage and generally accepted the word "world" here to mean that God so loved people. But the original language there for "world" is *kosmos*. The passage does not say "for God so loved humans, or people." No, *kosmos* refers to the entirety of creation. We have to take note here that when God talks about his plan of renewal and offering the greatest sacrifice, His Son, He had **all** of creation in mind.

Remember back to Genesis when sin first entered creation. Sin impacted everything. It wasn't just the humans. The ground was harder to till. Plants were impacted. Animals were affected. There was no part of creation that remained untouched by the brokenness. So, it makes sense that God's plan would make **all** things whole again.

Now consider this: this word *kosmos* in John 3:16 is the same word used by Mark for "world" in his version of the great commission: "He said to them, 'Go into all the world and preach the gospel to all creation'" (Mark 16:15 NASB). Jesus deployed His disciples to share the good news of His work with the entire *kosmos* and *ktisis* ("creation," in Greek). Jesus wanted His messengers to have an impact on everything.

Another part of the problem is that we have unfortunately translated the original word *kerysso* from the great commission passage as "preach."[5] This makes us think living the great commission looks like giving a lot of sermons. That's not exactly what Jesus meant. A better translation of this word *kerysso* in the Mark passage is "**herald, or someone that proclaims openly what has occurred.**"

In Jesus' time, whenever a new emperor would take power, the Roman government would send out messengers and riders to all the towns to make the announcement. These heralds would arrive, with the dust cloud still blowing from under the horses' feet, and say, "Hear the *gospel*, the good news, that Caesar Augustus is the new emperor." Sound familiar? In essence, they were declaring that the people had no reason to fear: the good news of the new ruler meant he will provide for them and protect the nation.

It is in this cultural context that Jesus calls His followers to be heralds who ride into all of creation to declare a new sort of news—that a new king is in power. But this king is unlike any other ruler the world has ever seen. This kingdom is marked by love, repentance, grace, and hope. And not just that, but Jesus' kingdom stands over and above every other kingdom on earth. The old has gone and the new has come—this is *new creation*.

As Wright puts it in *Simply Jesus*:

What we are witnessing in the resurrection stories . . . is the birth of new creation. The power that has tyrannized the old creation has been broken, defeated, overthrown. God's kingdom is now launched, and launched in power and glory, on earth as in heaven.[6]

Wright opens up this theme of new creation further by bringing our attention to the opening phrase of John 20. This is the moment when John unveils the resurrection, and as he shares the incredible story of the empty tomb, he begins by saying: "Now on the first day of the week Mary Magdalene came to the tomb early, while it was still dark" (John 20:1 NASB).

On the first day of the week.

For John, this is not just an introductory throwaway phrase. John is actually anchoring the radical news of the resurrection he is about to share straight back to Genesis and the creation story. To the story of sin, betrayal, separation, and now the climax of that narrative when all things are restored in the person of Jesus. For John, the first day of the week means the first day of God's *new* week and the launching of *new creation*.[7]

God's work through the cross is just as much for today as it is for our future eternity. Jesus' new kingdom has finally arrived on earth. The prophecies have become reality, and now, He has handed the reins to His followers to make His kingdom flourish everywhere. His plan all along was to use His united people to unleash the enormous restorative power of the Gospel. This should shatter a golden ticket faith mentality and point to the greater work God has done and is doing. There is no room for such shallow thinking when our King has won the victory and has now released us to go implement that victory. Today. Here and Now.

What good is the reconciliation power of the Gospel we so dearly love if we do not allow it to do its full work among us first? How can we be the ambassadors and heralds Christ calls us to be if we have not yet allowed the power of the message to do its work in our own fellowship? This is why we love and celebrate the cross; it is the place where we receive grace.

This means we have work to do. Fun, challenging, and life-giving work. If we see the greater design that we are conduits for His will, then we will immediately see how we need one another. So vast are the problems and so critical is our mission that not one congregation, one person, or one organization could ever tackle it all alone. However, if the Church could recognize our mutual need and operate *as one*, we would be the most formidable force for good. New creation would spring up all around us.

SYSTEMS THINKING

Another key way we need to change our thinking to recognize our interdependence and mutual need is learning how to see things in wholes: systems thinking.

Our universe is an amazing system. One stands in awe at just a few examples of creation: sunsets, mountains, animals, flowers, galaxies, and the human eye.

The individual elements are incredible, but maybe more amazing is the intricate interconnected tapestry of creation. If single pieces of our world were removed, the whole system would decay. Consider that just a few fractional changes in our distance from the sun would make life on earth impossible. The moon is also the perfect size to produce just enough gravitational pull to create important tides for marine life and the constraint of the oceans water. There is balance and harmony with the right proportions.

Although our world and universe are complicated systems, we fail to make this transition into how we think in our own lives. The Western mental "toolkit" generally teaches us to abstract things from their whole, elevating ideas of individualism and competition.

Systems thinking works to counteract that.

Learning this new discipline is all about seeing the "forest *and* the trees" or seeing the "starling *and* the Murmuration." Systems thinking is actually a science that provides a new way to think and view the world, allowing us to see the big picture and the interconnectedness of seemingly unrelated things.[8] The systems thinking field is broad and can be applied to many arenas: social, biological, business. Many great minds from Harvard and MIT have contributed to this incredible science over the years, and we have much to learn from these brilliant leaders. For our purposes here, we barely scratch the surface on how systems thinking principles could shape the Church toward unity.

Like most disciplines, it is so critical not because of the discipline itself, but because of what the discipline *produces*. Although not typically applied to the Church, the lessons systems thinking offers for those who follow Jesus can profoundly change our view of the Church and produce the perspective we need for unity to flourish.

Peter Senge, a thought leader in the field, points out that human endeavors are systems that:

> are bound by invisible fabrics of interrelated actions, which often take years to fully play out their effect on each other. Since we are part of that lacework ourselves, it's doubly hard to see the whole pattern of change.

Instead, we tend to focus on snapshots of isolated parts of the system, and wonder why our deepest problems never seem to get solved.[9]

The Church is indeed also such a system, an organization made up of many smaller sub-organizations. But since we are a part of the system ourselves, we do not typically see it as a whole. In the back of our minds, the idea might exist that we are one greater body, but how often is it lived out practically?

The central challenge is to change the way we see ourselves and the world around us. Learning to see things in wholes will help us think correctly and see the interrelationships between things rather than just isolated units. When applied, this discipline will destroy the illusion that the world is created of separate, unrelated forces or that God's Church is just a loose network of independent local churches.[10] Like any discipline, learning and practicing it is difficult. This discipline will be particularly hard to learn with the frenetic pace we keep because it requires slowing down to see the gradual processes at play. It will take a lot of time—that means it will also require patience.

It even takes time for the experts. Jay Forrester, considered to be one of the fathers of system dynamics, once undertook a project with John Collins, retired Boston mayor. Their aim was to look systematically at urban cities and draw insights about poverty, housing, crime, and more. Even for Forrester and the elite team of experts on cities that he and Collins gathered, this process took time. Despite living in different cities, this team of experts made an incredible commitment and gathered *every Wednesday afternoon for one year!* Sounds like a possible gathering of Seven Influential Neighbors. The discussions of that group were eventually developed into one of Forrester's books, *Urban Dynamics.*[11]

This is not a "fix it overnight" discipline, but it is the one we need if we want lasting change. It is as if we are stuck in a rip current and without knowing how the system of a rip current works, we don't understand that the solution is to swim sideways. We want to challenge you to think of the global Christian Church as a system. Just like creation, the Church is an interconnected tapestry made up of many parts, designed to reflect God's glory. As John Armstrong says, we currently have a limited and narrow view of the Church.[12] We agree. It is time to slow down so we can learn this game-changing discipline. It will reveal a new picture showing us the leverage we possess, paving the way to build real momentum for unity.

For the Church, we must recognize our mutual need for one another. Consider that "in human systems, people often have potential leverage that they do not exercise because they focus only on their own decisions and ignore how their decisions affect others."[13] Recall our discussion in chapter 2. The psychology of our "egocentric selves" causes us to think only about ourselves (or at least think of ourselves first). Not only does this go against the message of Christ to love others first, but according to systems thinking, this is also the major cause of lost leverage. This, of course, is compounded by the in-group/out-group way we think, and we subsequently lose concern for how the ripples we make in the water affect others. Let us remember that in Christ's new kingdom, "we are members one of another" (Ephesians 4:25 ESV). In the Christian walk, there is no such thing as *them*, there is just *we*. Systems thinking helps us start to actually think that way.

Learning to see things systematically is a process, but you will know it when you see it. Like the moment you suddenly see an optical illusion or a "magic eye" picture. At first you cannot see the image within the image, but then, like the flicking on of a switch, you see past what your brain told you at first and see the second image. Learning to think systematically is much like this activity and you will wonder, *How did I not see that before?*

The Church desperately needs these new types of thinkers. It all comes down to redefining our scope of influence, meaning that we see ourselves as part of the whole. May we allow Him to rewire the way we think, training us to see the value others bring. And may He show us how much we need others, taking off our blinders to see that our actions matter within the entire system.

Imagine buying the latest album from your favorite artist, only to find that instead of combining all the various instruments into one fluid song, they took a shortcut and only released tracks of each individual instrument by themselves. You are now supposed to figure out how to put them together and in what order. Track one, just bass. Track two, just background vocals. Track three, cowbell. Imagine how empty it would sound to have only the individual parts. The tracks need one another to become the beautiful song they were intended to be.

For us, it is difficult to admit how much we need others. Sometimes the spotlight from a solo feels good, or dependence can make us feel weak or less than adequate. But look at it this way: if the Christian community is "through Jesus Christ and in Jesus Christ" as the famous theologian Bonhoeffer taught us, then this means that "Christians need others because of Jesus Christ." In other words, we belong to one another and

> If we are designed to be Christ to each other, yet we cannot recognize our need for all our brothers and sisters, then we must ask ourselves if, ultimately, we cannot recognize our need for God.

are quite literally Christ in the flesh to each other as Christ lives in us.[14] So, if we are designed to be Christ to each other, yet we cannot recognize our need for all our brothers and sisters, then we must ask ourselves if, ultimately, we cannot recognize our need for God.

God is so gracious and patient. But He is still waiting, longing for His children to repent and forgive one another. Waiting for us to understand how much we truly need each other. Yearning for His children to realize their full potential and operate at the levels He designed us for. God is earnestly awaiting the heralding of His kingdom to all creation. Let's not keep Him waiting any longer.

Chapter 8

Principle 5: There Is No Alpha

Our Christian destiny is, in fact, a great one: but we cannot achieve greatness unless we lose all interest in being great.
—Thomas Merton[1]

The Murmuration is one of the most unmatched displays of collective behavior. Although you might imagine that every bird is following a chain of command, consider this: there is no solitary leader in a Murmuration. With no central operations control, no star celebrity leader or top-down hierarchy, *any single bird can initiate a Murmuration.*[2]

Not only can any bird *start* a Murmuration, but any solitary starling can also change the direction of the entire flock once it is in flight. Birds at the front can quickly be at the back when a sweep changes the direction of the flock. If a bird banks, its influence ripples through the entire Murmuration like a wave. Amazingly, the flock usually responds only when birds bank *into* the flock, rather than away. If a bird leads *away* from the flock, there is usually little or no response.[3] These responses diminish the risk of being picked off by a predator because the flock rules keep everyone together and allow for exceptionally rapid reactions. To accomplish this, they must be intensely aware of their Seven Influential Neighbors and respond appropriately to those around them. Without a singular leader, global order still emerges.

Even with the most elite levels of leadership within human organizations, collective behavior remains an extremely elusive challenge. For the starlings, however, collective movement is as natural as breathing. Even without an alpha, a Murmuration comes to life as the leadership mantle gets passed effortlessly among the flock. *For the Murmuration to explode, the key is not found in following one bright light leader, but rather in the interaction within individual relationships.* This is the key to their unity and extremely fast sharing of information.[4]

Think about groups where there is one central leader and everyone follows that commander. With this model, there is usually a high level of order, but very little interaction between individuals. This means a minimized transfer of information between individuals; if one person makes a movement, it has very little impact on the overall group. Therefore, when it comes time for a hierarchical group like this to respond to something, self-organized collective movement becomes impossible—everyone is just waiting for the alpha to lead.

On the other hand, groups with no central command typically do not have a high level of order, but have heavy interaction between individuals. The Murmuration is extraordinary because it is still able to achieve a high level of order without status, a single leader, or centrality of authority. The lack of hierarchy does not produce anarchy. The starlings are not driven by the individualism necessary for anarchy. Although there is no alpha, however, the movement still needs leadership, which comes within the formation.

The application of these findings is paramount for us. We aim for this unity in our businesses and communities, but most of the time we employ the top-down approach of leadership. **The principle we learn here breaks that paradigm: our ability to walk in unity depends on leadership, and *any single one of us* has the power to lead.**

You have significance. There may be moments when you feel you're without purpose, direction, or influence, but the truth is that God has placed something inside of you to offer the Church and our world. In the Church, we've complicated things with brands, alpha leaders, power, and money. We've become concerned at times with being great instead of making *Him* great. In essence, our childish perspectives and inability to see Christ's vision have propelled us into embracing less—much less. God doesn't love us less in those moments of weakness, but He does grieve our lost power and efficiency because we are operating outside of our design.

> Our ability to walk in unity depends on leadership, and any single one of us has the power to lead.

We are significant and yet, it's not about us. It's not about our organization or who gets the credit for anything. It is time that those who claim Christ as King see this vision, rise up, and lead. Let's mutiny against the current status quo of division in the Church. Every single one of us can be initiators. It is not the responsibility of our pastor, a famous influencer, or anyone else—we are all part of the flock. The responsibility belongs to *all* of us and we cannot wait any longer; the world cannot wait any longer. In disunity, the Church is limping along—but if each of us saw our potential to lead and spark a movement, then the floodgates of heaven would burst wide open.

You have the power to initiate the movement in your community. Like any vision, becoming a murmurating church will require leadership—your leadership. God has placed into the Murmuration extraordinary parallels with His concept of the Church: one body with multiple members. If one member hurts, the whole body hurts. If one member changes direction, the whole body banks that way. If one celebrates, we all celebrate. Unity is harmony in action.

But what good is it to believe that Jesus designed us for this unity and then do nothing about it? Will you choose this day to bank with the flock and cast a vision to your neighboring Christians about biblical unity?

WHAT KIND OF LEADERSHIP?

We know from experience that triggering unity, lasting partnerships, collaboration, or unified strategies are all dependent on committed leadership and individuals stepping up.[5] Someone has to pick up the phone, send an email, cast the vision, make the invitation, or call a meeting.

Stepping up means being aware of where you fit into the fabric of the Church in your community to meet the most appropriate need that fits your gifts and strengths. In 1 Corinthians it is clear that every believer has been given different gifts. Through our specific gifting, we have a place of optimal efficiency in that area. We were each designed with a specific purpose in mind, but also designed to offer our strengths in the context of community. Taking initiative means connecting the dots on how our gifts interplay with our neighbors who also follow Jesus.

In the Church, there will be no migration toward unity without resolute leadership, leadership that points us to bigger and better playgrounds, to our true design, which shows the Church how to transition to heights we never thought possible. You may not identify yourself as a "leader," but you can still influence in some way. Big or small, in the background or onstage, we all have a role to play.

From our experience, the following characteristics are key elements that must be settled into the hearts of the movement's leaders. This is the DNA for the *kind* of leadership we need for a Murmuration movement in the Church: bold, compassionate, vision-based, focused, and empowering.

1. We Need Bold Leadership

When Jesus saw the abuse of the merchants and moneylenders in the temple, the only reason He stopped for a moment was so he could make a whip for driving everyone out (John 2:15)! Matthew 21 recounts the same story, telling us about Jesus' bold leadership as He turned over the tables. Jesus knew what was right and He didn't care what cultural norm He had to break to take the right action. I am sure there was a certain fire in His eyes that caused the real fear in the onlookers—a passion and zeal for the Lord that was more awe-inspiring than the scene itself.

We need this sort of bold leadership to carry a dynamic passion for unity into the Church. We need leaders who are not afraid to take action and flip the tables on the realities we have settled for. These leaders are willing to put their reputation on the line, knowing they stand for something that matters to God—and the opinions of man hold no power. This sort of bold leadership might require you to have difficult conversations or challenge those in your network by calling out in love the sin of division. We are not Jesus—so be careful not to judge the heart and accuse people of wrong motives. They may have wrong motives, but that is up to God to convict—focus on the fruit and facts of what actions are producing. This sort of bold leadership will also require you to forgive others and choose grace, mercy, and unity in difficult circumstances.

This boldness should come from the confidence in knowing God's design, and knowing that we have to operate there, or we will miss so much.

2. *We Need* Compassionate *Leadership*

A compassionate leader is one who can relate to others, can walk a mile in their shoes, and can see things through the lens of the "other." This leader is also filled with grace toward others even if they do not agree. Boldness and passion must be tempered by compassion—to hurt and to celebrate with others.

A compassionate leader does not take control because of his or her position; he or she leads by example with integrity and is patient with others when they don't see the vision for unity as clearly as this leader does. Remember that everyone is on his or her own growth trajectory. In the same way it took time to catch the vision for yourself, it will take time for others.

Compassionate leadership also requires a servant's heart. It is a realization, as 1 Corinthians teaches, that the whole point of our gifts is to serve and benefit the body—not to boost ourselves up. Jesus' ministry on earth came at a great personal cost. He not only let go of His glory to take the form of a man, He lived to serve others to the point of death.

What sort of leader are you? Do you use your position to promote yourself, gain wealth, popularity, fame, or platform? Or are you a leader who is willing to give till it hurts for the sake of the Body? When your dedication to the mission starts to truly cost you something, you will know you are beginning to serve as Christ served.

3. *We Need* Vision-Based *Leadership*

When Jesus offered bold leadership in driving out the money-lenders from the temple, He quickly anchored His actions in Scripture: He said to them, "It is written, 'My house shall be called a house of prayer,' but you make it a den of robbers" (Matthew 21:13 ESV). He pointed His audience to Scripture and legitimized His bold actions with the vision.

If our leadership doesn't continually point people to the vision or the cause, everything quickly becomes about those in leadership. This is where Jim Collins draws the line between what he calls "level 4" and "level 5" leadership. Level 4 leaders can successfully get people to follow *them*. Level 5 leaders are able to successfully get people to follow a *cause*.[6] This is the art of getting people to *want* to do what needs to be done.

Without a clear theological framework, we lose our boldness to radically live in unity. All of our actions as leaders must be deeply rooted in the vision. But this is not just an internal process. We also have to show those around us *how* our actions are rooted in the vision. This is what vision-based leadership is. We use our influence to continually re-cast the biblical vision and passion, reminding the world *why* we do what we do. This might feel redundant or get old at times. However, vision-based leadership over-communicates the vision to keep everyone motivated.

4. *We Need* Empowering *Leadership*

The birds in a Murmuration do not hold tightly to their leadership. There is no battle in this flock for positioning or territory. In a grassroots unity movement for the Church, our leaders will also have to hold on to their leadership loosely (to clarify, we're not talking about ministry staff positions). You could be the initiator of a God-sized idea today, but then tomorrow it could be someone else. We have to be ready to empower and release leadership to other believers because it is not about the position we hold, but rather how we can serve others *through* the position.

In fact, we should enthusiastically look for those we can raise up to lead beside us or behind us. This is empowering leadership— leadership that is not only okay with losing a position, but proactively works to release and empower others to lead.

Jesus led this way. He entrusted the entire Gospel movement to His followers and empowered us with the Holy Spirit. There was no other plan or major marketing campaign, just people— His groups of friends, disciples, and followers. He told them: *Go into the world and make disciples, just like I showed you—and if you want to be any good at all at making disciples for my glory, then fight for unity at all costs. The power of the movement depends on it. The world will know you are truly my disciples by the love among you, and through that unity, they will see that I am truly the Son of God.*

Our cultural default is that if you want it done right, you have to do it yourself. But consider what Jesus was able to accomplish by releasing and empowering His followers. In three years, he took a group of rugged fishermen and taught them how to be *just like Him* so that when sent out, they would change the course of human history forever.

The way Jesus wants His movement to run is simply this: people sharing life with other people. This is how the movement becomes replicable. If everything hinges on one incredible and inspiring alpha leader, what happens when that person moves on? It is possible to make great strides toward unity in a community, but if only a single leader is willing to step up, the movement will suffer if that person ever moves. Leading in a way that empowers others helps get the vision to critical mass and anchor it into a community because more people are taking ownership.

The movement will grow only when empowered leaders begin replicating and empowering other leaders. The passion for unity among the Church in your community will not grow simply from one person being the strong voice. The Jesus way is apprenticeship, empowerment, and release.

In *Building a Discipling Culture*, Breen and Cockram explain that the discipleship process in its simplest form follows this flow: Information—Imitation—Innovation.[7] In the West, we are heavy on teaching and typically stay stuck in the *information* phase, thinking that knowledge is discipleship. We rarely give others full access to our lives for them to imitate from watching and learning outside of a classroom setting. For apprenticeship to really grow, information must flow into an *imitation* phase when we lead by example. The last step is to release others to *innovate* on their own with what they have learned from you.

An empowering leader will take others through this flow in order to replicate champions for the movement.

MIKE'S STORY

One of the challenges facing networks and movements for unity is when the strong voices leave the table. These "loud voices" are the leaders who have championed the idea of unity and have called others to the table. Maybe they have led the way in strategic planning and casting vision, but for healthy reasons they move away when they are called to another ministry. What happens then?

Recently at a network that meets at Biola University, we had four very strong leaders transition out of our network. Most of them had moved into new positions of ministry in their present churches and their focus was changing. It was a real blow to our network. Not only were their voices gone but their hearts and passion for unity too.

The challenge now was to inspire new voices to step up, speak out, and lead where the others have left off. What I witnessed was an exciting evolution of leadership. It was a joy to see others use their leadership gifts and take up new positions of leadership.

5. *We Need* Focused *Leadership*

According to Collins, great leadership is "not just about humility and modesty. It is equally about ferocious resolve, an almost stoic determination to do whatever needs to be done."[8] Being a compassionate and humble leader is key, but those attributes must be paired with an unwavering will to move forward.

We see this sort of leadership in Daniel 3 from Hananiah, Mishael, and Azariah, or better known by their pagan names: Shadrach, Meshach, and Abednego. As the story goes, King Nebuchadnezzar built a huge golden statue and decreed that everyone must worship the idol, but these three faithful leaders from the tribe of Judah would not bow down. In the face of certain death, threatened to be thrown into a furnace, they remained focused with fierce determination on what was really important. It would have been easy in that moment to make an emotional case for why a small compromise would be understandable. Instead, we see bold and focused leadership. They were vocal about what they believed and despite being given the opportunity, they did not allow the momentary circumstances to distract them from the bigger picture.

The Murmuration movement in the Church will need leaders who stay stubbornly focused on unity. It may even get irritating to some, but focused leaders will not back down.

Why would we? If the greatest leverage and power for the mission of the Church lies in our unity, then this is worth being relentlessly focused on. Remember, there will be noise and limiting factors that arise. The leader's role will be to reduce the possibility of the movement derailing in any way. This is why a focused leader will generate enough trust and momentum *in advance* of any speed bumps so that conflict, miscommunication, and any other limiting factors will not stop the movement.

WHO WE ARE = WHAT WE DO (AND NOT THE OTHER WAY AROUND)

Who we are is absolutely foundational. Leading toward unity and collective movement begins with the state of our hearts, not in strategy or what we do. We have to get our hearts right first. From who we are overflows what we do and how we do it. In this chapter, we covered first the *kind* of leadership we need, the *who* we are along the way: bold, compassionate, vision-based, empowering, focused.

Now we offer a few practical steps for where to start as a leader for unity. Remember this is a dynamic process, so perfection is not a prerequisite before we actually do anything; the point is knowing that the heart comes first. If we get the **what** correct, but miss the **who** behind anything we do, we'll be stuck wondering why we are hitting so many roadblocks. Only from an overflow of the heart should we pursue the pragmatic nuts and bolts of what to do as ambassadors for unity in the Church.

We will expand more on the practical steps for what a community-wide strategy and momentum can look like in chapter 12, but if you are ready to help get the movement to a tipping point, here are six practical things you can do to lead:[9]

1. Prayerfully Find Your Seven Influential Neighbors and Challenge Them to Do the Same

Following the ideas laid out in chapter 4, identify a diverse group of Seven Influential Neighbors. If you have a specific project you are working on, prayerfully find seven strategic and diverse people who might fit the project. If you do not have something specific, start meeting with seven other believers simply to build relationships.

Remember, these groups are not designed to be new cliques or permanent exclusive groups. The Seven Influential Neighbors group is not a rigid prescription—we are a body that is dynamic and flowing. Starlings have many different influential neighbors, so consider challenging your Seven Influential Neighbors to put together their own group as well to multiply the vision.

2. Share God's Vision and Our Current Reality Constantly and Publicly

With the trust that comes through relationships, share the biblical vision for unity and a clear picture of our current state of division. There was a moment that God showed you His greater design, so now create the space where God can take the blinders off for your friends.

Since Christ directly correlated the unity of the Church with the world knowing He is the true Son of God, it is critical that we make our unity public. *Remember the point of unity is not only unity itself, but also what unity produces.* We cannot only share the message to our small groups behind closed doors. We have to let the greater community see our love and our collective movement.

Even if our efforts are not perfect, consistently communicating what we are doing and why we are doing it will begin the slow process of changing the way believers and non-believers see the Church. This constant vision casting in our church, organization, and community will also generate the creative tension believers need.

3. Establish a Sense of Urgency

We don't have a moment to lose. The world is hurting, lost, and in desperate need of God's love. We have the answers our world craves, yet our potential to accomplish the mission has been severely stifled. As long as we are fragmented, our God-given calling will continue to suffer. Disunity is the dam that holds back the mission of the Church; only unity will burst the floodgates wide open.

> Disunity is the dam that holds back the mission of the Church; only unity will burst the floodgates wide open.

This truth should naturally produce a sense of desperation to unite among Christ followers, but we must also communicate this message with urgency. Our message must be clear and consistent: unity is critically important to Christ, and the Church is missing key leverage by remaining in disunity.

The easiest way to develop urgency is to communicate the need and the possibilities constantly. Think of how many hungry, lonely, lost, abandoned, and sick people in the world are still hurting because our disunity has weakened our mission. Think of God's heart—broken that His children are fighting, and all the while His great message of reconciliation is undermined when the messengers are unreconciled. We must cultivate urgency in ourselves and the Body of Christ around us.

4. Let Creativity Explode

Knowing the vision, creating urgency, and seeing our current reality have one result: an explosion of creativity. The graph

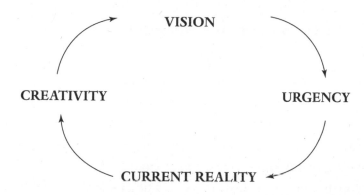

Creativity loop (Lucas Ramirez)

above depicts the process of how knowing God's design causes urgency for the mission. Despite seeing the design, in life we quickly hit our reality and realize how far we are from the vision. Many times, the movement loses energy here and stops. If we can push past the negative emotions from seeing our current reality, however, the vision, urgency, and reality wrangle together to create a near nuclear chemistry of creativity for solving our most pressing problems.

This loop is not a man-made effort, so dependence on the Holy Spirit is critical. Always start (and re-start) with the biblical vision or else human creativity will drive the vision. With human eyes, our tendency is to control the process when creativity begins to explode. Sometimes the ideas are radical, dangerous, disruptive, or come from unexpected sources. It is true that not all ideas need to be implemented, but we must be careful not to squelch the creativity too soon. If all of this is done within diversity, the creativity that would otherwise have been impossible will inspire everyone involved.

5. Invite Others into the Movement and Empower Them for Action

Once the vision is cast with urgency and creativity is flourishing among a small core of committed leaders, this is the time to fling the doors wide open and build the critical mass. As the vision grows in your own backyard, help others catch the wave by freely apprenticing other leaders with the vision and release them to do the same. You can do this by inviting someone to a meeting of your Seven Influential Neighbors. Give someone a copy of this book. Blog on unity or post Scriptures that highlight God's heart for unity. Tell stories of unlikely people coming together in unity for something greater. Building critical mass and inviting others to the vision do not have to be complicated.

Remember that we need empowering leadership and you can be a champion for unity anywhere. *Someone* has to lead. Even if you are not the top leader within an organization, you can still champion unity. Effective partnerships need a champion inside every organization to do what needs to be done.[10] You are an important part of God's plan to multiply the kingdom.

6. Celebrate Victories and Anchor Changes into the Culture of Your Community and Organization

Once a *Murmuration* takes flight, no single individual is in control and a greater power is at work. This is the time to ride the wave and celebrate all that God is doing! Maybe new partnerships or collaborative projects have birthed. Maybe relationships have been reconciled or new relationships have emerged.

We need to stop and celebrate these wins. We can do this by telling stories of forgiveness over bitterness. We can do this by preaching sermons on healing across racial lines. We can do this by calling the newspaper and asking them to write a story on collaborative partnerships. You can also do this by going to our website and sharing your story of how God moved powerfully through unity in your community (www.DesignedFor MoreBook.com). We need not be afraid of bragging when it comes to showing the world our migration toward unity. This is the time to shamelessly boast about what God is doing and make unity public.

It is critical to rejoice over any victories, big or small. This helps us remember that God is at work. This storytelling will play a major role in anchoring the movement into the hearts of believers. Unity can be very abstract, but when we can see tangible examples of unity at work, it gives us a helpful mental framework. This is also part of anchoring the changes in our organizations because they change our way of thinking. Converting a single event into a culture-changing force within a community is possible. It requires celebrating the wins, talking about them, debriefing together, dissecting, and drawing out the lessons learned. Making time for this process together is the difference between an event in time and a culture-changing victory.

Leaders answering this call for unity lead a living organism, not a static organization. Big ideas require constant attention, and bringing together a fractured church is certainly no exception. The life of the movement depends on your leadership.

Will you step up?

The universal Church needs local leaders, everyday believers, and high-profile leaders to all take on this yoke of leadership toward unity. If the champions of ministry would champion unity, that could change the face of the Church. We need key stakeholders at every level to catch the passion and lead publicly and loudly so everyone will notice.

One great paradox in the Church is that we are both traditional and revolutionary. Human traditions and revolutions wither, stall, or simply pass power to the next regime. All other worldly revolutions call for the death of someone else or something else, but the revolution of the Gospel calls for the death of your own self.[11] The leaders we need are the individuals willing to lay their life down and be living sacrifices for God and their neighbors. On the other side of this spiritual baptism, a refined and renewed person will emerge, ready to lead with power in the way God designed.

To build any significant momentum for a Murmuration to sweep through the Church, it will require this sort of resurrected leader. The movement is waiting for you to step up and influence your community. This is a massive project, worthy of all we have to offer, but it is not for the faint of heart. In your corner of the world, be bold, compassionate, releasing, vision-based, and focused. Now lead!

Chapter 9

Principle 6: Divide You Die

Any kingdom divided against itself will be ruined, and a house divided against itself will fall.

—Luke 11:17 NIV

The power of the Murmuration is in the numbers. But it's not just quantity that matters. Thousands of scattered or disorganized birds have no collective power, but it is the *unified* number that makes all the difference.

For the starlings, they are most vulnerable when isolated. The moment a member of the flock splits off, it becomes the target of its predator; if you divide you die. Their elite predators are on watch, waiting for the starlings that wander off from the flock. According to Murmuration expert Anne Goodenough, "Most aerial predators hunt by targeting a specific bird within a group," and the constant movement within the Murmurations do not allow the predators to lock on to a target.[1] When a starling begins to divide from the group, it falls prey to the attack of its enemies.

There are both internal and external forces that work to divide a Murmuration. Some starlings might have a screw loose or didn't inherit the right instincts and decide to split off from the flock. Other times, exterior conditions like heavy rain, wind, and snow can impact the Murmuration. These external factors can impede the phenomenon by limiting visibility or slowing down the transfer of information between the birds. Despite these limiting factors within and without, however, the starlings understand the importance of sticking together. As long as the birds stay true to their nature and design, they will seek unity. Separation means death. So regardless of the circumstances that arise to divide them, they fight to stay together.

In the Church, we have so many tough circumstances and disagreements that give us reasons to split. Just a quick look at recent history shows major mainline denominations dividing over doctrinal issues. Despite having the same ultimate purpose, others split over diverse perspectives on outreach strategies and missiology. A glance at current headlines shows the raging debates and tension around race and sexual ethics. Our apathy or unwillingness to forgive and learn from those in an "opposing" tribe becomes an internal contributor that only feeds the external schisms. It is a corruption to the very nature of the Church.

I know what you might be thinking: *false teaching is a corruption to the Church.* We don't disagree. For a few brief moments, however, suspend that thought and read on to enhance your perspective of how we can balance God's call for truth and unity.

We have to begin again by acknowledging that we've lost our true nature and design to be one collective body. We were created to be 100 percent in community and remain 100 percent an individual. The Church is the only community in the world designed to keep the individuality of each person, while at the same time learning to live with "the other" in community. This is the master plan and anchor for how our fellowship can reflect God to the world. Our sinful nature, however, has distorted this blueprint for community when disunity takes root in the heart of the individual. This internal idolatry then manifests into many external factors that split our community. It might not be rain, snow, or wind, but when slander, fear, and jealousy are in the forecast, the enemy has us right where he wants us. We split for "good" reasons, yet we forget too easily that separation means death for us too.

Our differences are highlighted even more today through the vast information at our fingertips. Repeated stories of division anchor yet again the wrong narrative that a divorced Church is the status quo. This reinforces the idea that our differences are so great and numerous that working toward unity is futile. The lack of effort to move in harmony is an affront to the very nature we were created for!

A book that invites us to live Christ's vision and design for unity would have a noticeable gap without a brief conversation on how to move forward *despite our differences*. Differences are real, cannot be ignored, and can be one of the major limiting factors to unity. God's intention is not to collect a group of spineless individuals who simply rally around a sort of lowest-common-denominator; that is not community, that is conformity. Our faith communities need some help in how to think about unity in the face of differences that feel like impassable chasms. In our limited space here, we want to offer a few ideas and signposts that we hope will guide us in the right direction.

Before we go any further, we need to state again a clearer definition of biblical unity. Biblical unity is *not* when everyone agrees on everything, mechanically falling in line. As we touched on previously, **unity is when all followers of Jesus realize their interconnectedness and pursue the oneness as seen in the Triune God in order to become one with God and each other—for His glory and the expansion of His kingdom.** Unity is intensely connected with the missional nature of our community because the point is not only our unity, but also what unity *produces*! This should give us hope for moving past our differences.

Our differences are so many, aren't they? Some are rooted in preferences, difference of strategy, or weighty like our view of Scripture and theology. Despite current divisions and any negative storylines, we challenge you to allow radical optimism to take root in your heart, even in the face of our differences.

As the theologian Padilla points out, "Membership in the body of Christ is not a question of likes or dislikes, but a question of incorporation into a new humanity under the lordship of Christ."[2] In the new covenant, Christ showed us a new way to be human where through the waters of baptism, we are resurrected into a new reality where cultural and ideological enemies can actually be reconciled and baptized into one body (1 Corinthians 12:13). Being baptized into this new body means dying to our idols and coming into a life where our differences become secondary to our identity in Christ.

The unity that Christ offers moves us beyond our cultural or doctrinal party lines. Consider that in Christ, the cultural norms in the ancient world were turned upside down. Jesus blurred their dividing lines: "There is neither Jew nor Greek, there is neither slave nor free, there is no male and female, for you are all one in Christ Jesus" (Galatians 3:28 ESV). God's truth lifts us beyond our cultural norms. It is hard for us to relate, but just imagine the enormous cultural concessions that the early church Jews had to make to welcome their new Gentile brothers and sisters in Christ. Enormous differences had to be put aside to accommodate the bigger mission, namely declaring Christ as king, savior, and healer of the world.

This chapter is our contribution to the conversation for how to move forward in unity despite very real differences. There *is* a biblical formula to accomplish this. We offer the following signposts to follow as we allow the Holy Spirit to lead us back to the original intent for our missional community. We share these thoughts in humility and love, with the greatest optimism that the Church has greater potential than we are now exercising.

SIGNPOST 1: EXPAND YOUR DEFINITION OF A PURE CHURCH

Has our definition of a *pure* church been too small?

Christians have made countless lists over the centuries of what constitutes a *pure* church. The search has not been for a *perfect* church (because such a thing does not exist), rather more of seeking the most holy and God-glorifying church possible. These lists have included key elements like sacraments, faith, authority, and morality. The problem is that in our lists of defining the nature and practice of a pure church, unity has rarely made the cut. Despite the overwhelming amount of Scripture inviting, commanding, and calling us to be one, somehow *unity* does not appear on our radar when defining a pure church. We've created a dichotomy where purity and unity stand opposed to one another, leaving us in a position of feeling like we have to choose between either one or the other.

We've landed in this either/or dilemma because of our historical and cultural positions. Historically, we are at the end of a timeline filled with splintering. For the first thousand years of church history, there was only one Church. It was not until the eleventh century that the Roman Catholic and Eastern Orthodox traditions created two parallel tracks. Then, the next major split happened through the Reformation in the sixteenth century with Protestants splitting off from the Catholic Church. That of course eventually led to the further splintering into the thirty thousand worldwide denominations we have today. Then culturally (predominantly in the West), we tend to elevate the individual and take a binary approach to reality, promoting this dichotomy between unity and purity. Without a clear understanding of our historical position or our Western cultural framework, this creates a dangerous combination.

It is time we expand our definition of a pure church to **include** unity as a major component. An overwhelming amount of Scripture shows that for Jesus and Paul, unity is a critical piece of a pure Church, so therefore, biblically, the Church cannot be pure without unity. **It is self-contradictory to fight for purity in the Church and sacrifice unity in the process.**

There is, no doubt, a clear biblical mandate to protect

It is self-contradictory to fight for purity in the Church and sacrifice unity in the process.

the Church. Truth matters and guarding the Church is an important part of caring for God's household, no matter if we are pastors, ministry staff, church members, or lay leaders. We have to take note, however, that when the Scriptures call us to fight for church purity, it is actually contextually tied to unity.

In the book of Titus, Paul calls us to silence false teachers (Titus 1:10–11) and at Paul's sharpest challenge, he says to "warn a divisive person once, and then warn them a second time. After that, have nothing to do with them. You may be sure that such people are warped and sinful; they are self-condemned" (Titus 3:10–11 NIV). Earlier in Romans, Paul urges the Church to "watch out for those who cause division and put obstacles in your way that are contrary to the teaching you have learned. Keep away from them. For such people are not serving our Lord Christ, but their own appetites" (Romans 16:17–18 NIV).

These and other similar passages are at times used to support splitting and dividing the Church. On the surface, without the complete context of Paul's teaching, it might be easy to interpret these passages as license to stick with our clusters of like-minded people. We cannot lose sight, though, that for Paul, the whole purpose of his exhortations in Titus and Romans is ultimately to protect unity in the body—and much less to open doors for splintering. If you look closely, the problem is the sinful nature in the individual and not the community. Paul is basically saying if someone makes the foolish decision to go against their design and bank away from the flock or try to divide the flock, you have to address it, because keeping the formation united is essential! Titus 2 calls us to be temperate and self-controlled, living in sight of God's grace, and in Titus 3, Paul commands us "to slander no one, to be peaceable and considerate, and always to be gentle toward everyone" (Titus 3:2 NIV). Yes, *everyone*.

Even if you're not yet convinced that Paul's exhortation in these passages is ultimately to protect unity, consider the waterfall of other passages that call us to unity. The Bible is slam full of them. To help you explore this theme in Scripture, we developed a free devotional and reading plan resource for you to download from our website—you can dive in by visiting: www.DesignedForMoreBook.com. You can also start your journey into what God is saying through these passages: Psalm 133:1–3; Ecclesiastes 4:9–12; Matthew 18:19–20; John 17; Acts 2:42–47; Romans 15:5–7; 1 Corinthians 1:10; 1 Corinthians 12:25; Ephesians 1:18, 4:1–6; Philippians 2:1–2; 1 Peter 3:8.

Two Pre-Suppositions Holding You Back

The big question that remains for many of us is: "How am I supposed to work with someone, or be *one* with another Christian, if they have such different perspectives from mine?" What we have to see first is that behind this valid question are two pre-suppositions: (1) there is a list of things that make you a *right* Christian and (2) *you* have that list perfectly ironed out. At the end of the day, if unity is essential to the purity of the Church, then this question is based on the wrong premise. We need to learn how to ask a different question.

Many times, we hesitate to work with others or be in relationship with them because of an issue that divides us. We are fighting for truth. But if we broadcast the importance of our perspective and lose unity in the process, we have defeated ourselves.

It *is* possible to be in fellowship with other believers who disagree on various issues, because Christian fellowship is not about being perfect before being accepted. It's quite the opposite. We are accepted and then made perfect through Christ. God didn't require the Israelites to be perfect and believe all the right doctrine before rescuing them from Egyptian slavery. He established His relationship with them *first* and then shared His design for the best life through the Ten Commandments.

It comes down to this: **it is hypocritical to have a high view of Scripture on an issue and sacrifice unity in the process as you fight for that issue.** *Both* unity and truth are biblical imperatives, so if we do not hold unity with all believers in high regard, that is in itself not holding a high view of Scripture. The real question we need to ask is: "How am I going to work with other believers and figure things out *in spite of* our differences?"

In a recent article, Dr. I Iinlicky Wilson says that in the Church

> There are many reasons for internal conflict, some sinful and some legitimate (though nearly everyone thinks their reasons are legitimate and only minimally sinful). But Paul makes an important distinction: While he acknowledges that "there must be factions among you in order that those who are genuine among you may be recognized" (1 Cor. 11:19, ESV), there must be "no divisions among you" (1:10).[3]

Paul's ecclesiology was able to hold this seeming paradox in balance. He was not stuck in the either/or dilemma of purity and unity that we struggle with. For Paul, having differences among believers and simultaneously taking seriously unity in the Church are not mutually exclusive positions.

God is full of cosmic-sized paradoxes. Perfect unity exists at the God level and although we can't create it with human effort, we can step into it. We are catalysts of it and protectors of it. Church, have we inadvertently given up the weightier things and higher points of leverage, while being distracted with fighting smaller battles? The point is *not* to show the world that all Christians fully agree on everything. The real beauty is to show that believers can be diverse, yet still united through the love of Christ because our unity is not based on culture or tradition, but rather based on Christ. This is how radically revolutionary and powerful His call to oneness is.

This is foundationally a new way to think for most of us, and this perspective will be critical if we are to move forward with Christ's vision despite our differences. Seeing unity as a central part of a pure Church is a key starting point and bridge across our many divides.

SIGNPOST 2: MAKE STRONG STATEMENTS, NOT STRONG ACCUSATIONS

Unity does not sacrifice truth. Today, postmodern culture has made truth a flexible human construct, defined by the individual. This is a dangerous place where the specific defines the universal. Evil is redefined as good and good whimsically redefined as evil. There is undoubtedly a battle for truth, and since Christians are messengers of the Truth, a lukewarm stance is not an option.

Where we miss-step is in our delivery. It is okay to make strong statements about your beliefs—in fact if you don't stand firmly for what you believe, it calls into question if you actually believe it. The key for believers (and where we get it wrong many times) is *how* we take a stand.

When we disagree, Christians tend to either accuse others of heresy, or we avoid those who we think don't like us, happy to have them go their own way. Neither of these responses promotes unity and our missional call. This is where we have to learn the skill of *dialogue* in relationship with our influential neighbors. As we explored earlier, there is a stark contrast between discussion and dialogue. Discussion is a debate, focused on an individual defending his or her own perspective. The point of a discussion is to win. On the other hand, the aim of dialogue is to learn. So often our public discourse is stuck in a discussion loop rather than the free exchange of ideas through dialogue.

We are not naturally born with the ability to dialogue. This is a skill that must be learned by watching and doing, observing others doing it effectively and practicing it ourselves.

To practice this skill, individuals must be (1) willing to listen to diverse perspectives and (2) able to suspend their own assumptions and evaluate them as if they were not their own.[4] This sort of collaborative dialogue will become richer over time. But it will require practice, reflecting, talking, and setting time aside to listen.[5] To become proficient in this skill, one must slow down and learn how to respond in humility and learn from other perspectives.

Although it may not feel like it, this process of dialogue rather than discussion is real progress toward unity. Research has shown that dialogue without consensus is still extremely beneficial because even though individuals may not agree, the process at least brings them to a mutual understanding of one another.[6] These are key steps in making "them" a part of "us" because when we understand others, we can more easily relate to them and love them.

To create a safe space for dialogue it will require:

- An assumption: the underlying belief that "I have not yet arrived"
- An environment: that encourages coming together and thinking out loud
- An openness: for feedback
- A commitment: that it's not about winning or taking sides
- A curiosity: listen and seek first to understand rather than be understood. Try responding with a question instead of a statement.

Notice that the practice of dialogue is not void of passion. Sparks might fly, but passion is delicately balanced with compassion. We should be comfortable making strong belief statements. It is okay for other believers to respond with strong statements that cause tension, but all in the context of dialogue. If you approach community with an agenda, there is little hope for achieving dialogue. Many times, our beliefs seem clear in our heart but can become unclear and contradictory when we express them. Dialogue is the opportunity to clarify what we believe in the context of community.

Proverbs 27:17 tells us that in a healthy relationship, friends sharpen one another, like iron sharpens iron. It is only extreme heat that makes iron pliable. Similarly, tension in our relationships can cause the friction and heat we need to be molded. The trick is to use this controlled fire to become pliable and teachable, not to cause quarrels and firestorms.

We must not get nervous when believers have clashing convictions. Remember, we can disagree and not sacrifice unity (as long as we get the *how* correct). This revelation hit me while jogging one day. I was almost three miles into my run when all of a sudden, I hit the proverbial "wall" and my muscles threw in the towel. I still had another stretch yet to run, so my mind and spirit were determined to finish. I had the mental will, but my physical body did not agree.

Your person is made up of mind, body, and spirit. To make you, God took diverse elements and fused them into one astounding masterpiece—you are beautiful! But just like me during my jog, there are times when your mind, body, and spirit disagree. We do not sacrifice unity or stop being one body in those moments of disagreement. In the Body of Christ, we are a family of diverse parts and we are called to stay in relationships even if we disagree. This is what you signed up for when you chose to follow Christ. It means not settling for discussion or squabbles on internet comment streams. It means fighting to find the correct platforms to have dialogue and share our perspectives. It means starting a new relationship with someone you can love, serve, and learn from.

Furthermore, it would be arrogant to think that our perspective is the correct one. Plato ascribed to Socrates, one of the originators of Greek dialogue as saying, "I know that I know nothing." This paradox gets to the idea that there is a lot that we do not know and a lot that we do not consider when we express our beliefs. Dialogue takes us to the point of humble acceptance that truth is much greater than what my beliefs have captured.

Undoubtedly, the issues we dialogue over are vitally important, but the issues that divide us are second in priority to

the *way* we respond to each other. What good is the truth of the Gospel if it does not change the way we live and treat one another? What substance does our message of reconciliation carry if we cannot be reconciled with one another? We cannot allow the issues that are so important to become idols. This is why 1 Corinthians 13:1 reminds us that "If I speak in the tongues of men and of angels, but have not love, I am only a resounding gong or a clanging cymbal" (NIV). Our mouths can be filled with the most eloquent apologetics and defense of truth, but if not soaked in love and grace, it is all meaningless. The inerrancy of Scripture, the divinity and humanity of Christ, the omnipotence of God, and the depravity of man all have no relevance if we do not deliver the message in a waterfall of love.

Love will change *how* we make the strong statements that need to be made. What if the key to solving the hot debates the Church faces is found in our ability to dialogue in love? Even the tone, spirit, and attitude behind how we disagree and how we communicate truth to the world deeply matter. It's like the front cover of a book. If the title and image don't captivate you, most readers will never get to the truth and content inside the book.

The theologian Richard Mouw coined the phrase "convicted civility" that speaks to this healthy way of relating to other believers. The idea is that people with strong convictions are often not very civil and people who are civil often don't have strong convictions.[7] *Convicted civility* is the ability to carry strong convictions and yet be civil with one another. You could also put it this way: *Do you love to tell the truth, or do you tell the truth in love?*

God did not release us to go into the world and change wrong theology. Only the work of the Holy Spirit can bring that conviction. He called us to go and love the world. When we encounter other believers who see things differently, the biblical signpost calls us to dialogue in humility and grace, not condemn. In the Murmuration, the starlings are not worried about their neighbor getting it right; they focus on getting it right themselves. Each starling follows their set of behavioral rules without trying to control those around them. It's not a matter of apathy for their neighbor; they just know they only have power to make their own decisions.

Practically, we can live this *convicted civility* by following steps offered by Dr. Brenda Salter McNeil from over twenty-five years of wisdom from working in reconciliation: (1) create safe spaces and use I statements like "I feel," or "I think"; (2) don't interrupt; (3) maintain confidentiality; and (4) be present.[8] These extremely practical steps make such a huge difference in the outcome of our conversations!

The world is hungry for Colossians 3 Christians: "Clothe yourselves with compassion, kindness, humility, gentleness and patience. Bear with each other and forgive one another if any of you has a grievance against someone. Forgive as the Lord forgave you. And over all these virtues put on love, which binds them all together in perfect unity" (Colossians 3:12–14 NIV). Unity is not for the faint of heart because it means forgiving seventy times seven, but the result will be an effervescent community working in the power of the Lord.

A Guiding Parable

In Luke 13, Jesus shares an incredible parable about a man who plants a fig tree and finds that it has not produced any fruit in the last three years. The man speaks to his vine keeper and tells him to cut down the fruitless tree. However, the vine-dresser responds by asking for time to till the ground around the tree, lay fertilizer, and see what happens after a year (Luke 13:6–9).

It is an interesting story. But what does it all mean? This short parable is critically central to our unity conversation and teaches us how to engage with one another. Theologians argue that this story is not actually about two different men; rather *it is about God having a conversation with Himself.* The gardener and owner each represent a different side of God—His mercy and justice. How can it be that God's justice and mercy can co-exist? This parable gives us a window into this mystery as it echoes Psalm 85, revealing what it's like when "justice and mercy kiss."

You see, we are the tree in the story. Fruitless, lost in sin, and deserving God's justice to be cut down. Despite what we deserve, God's mercy (the vinedresser), rises up and becomes our advocate: "Give the poor guy one more chance. This one needs a little extra help."

God balances both justice and mercy, the law and grace, truth with love. It is as if each represents a different foot—and rather than leading with the justice foot, He chooses to lead with mercy. He doesn't throw justice and truth away; they just don't take the lead. Jesus showed us the ultimate display of this type of love on the cross. As Volf says, "The cross is the result when God sets out to embrace his enemy."[9] In this one event, God co-mingled His mercy and justice in the greatest expression of sacrificial love.

So we, too, have two feet. We have the choice to lead with mercy or justice. And the first step desperately matters.

Have we forgotten that Jesus actually washed the feet of Judas just hours before Judas would betray Him? In John 13, we can miss a subtle but powerful message if we glance over verse two: "During supper, when the devil had already put it into the heart of Judas Iscariot, Simon's son, to betray him... He laid aside his outer garments, and taking a towel, tied it around his waist. Then he poured water into a basin and began to wash the disciples' feet and to wipe them with the towel that was wrapped around him" (John 13:2, 4–5 ESV). The Gospel writers wanted to make it very clear that *Jesus washed the feet of His betrayer, knowing full well the reality of what he would do.* Maybe this is what Psalm 23 really means when it says "you lay a table before me in the presence of my enemies" (NIV). As if this astounding display of leading with love were not enough, think about this: the last personal interaction Jesus had with Judas was to serve him communion (John 13:26).

Are you willing to wash the feet of those you disagree with? The slanderer in your life? The liar? Your "doctrinally wrong" Christian brother or sister? It is extremely difficult in the emotion of the moment, but when we are led by core values and God's design for unity, our principles will guide our behavior, not our emotions. Since we have been embraced by Christ, then embracing others who are different must be our response if we have fellowship with Christ. As the Galatians 3 passage teaches us, we see ourselves fully only when our primary identity is in Christ—as sons, daughters, and heirs, rather than in our education, degree, job, marriage, race, or culture. We're equally free and equally cherished because God doesn't have favorite children. Therefore, we're not rivals, but free to serve one another—even our enemy.

SIGNPOST 3: STICK TO THE CORE VALUES

There is a hilarious scene in the *Little Rascals* movie when their clubhouse is on fire. Mayhem ensues and the kids begin running around grabbing buckets of water, hoses, and calling for help. But then, for a brief second, the film focuses on a young boy who sat down to roast a marshmallow on the very fire that's burning the clubhouse!

I wonder if we are caught in a similar scene of hilarity and absurdity. With a world that has been set aflame by a barbarous and cruel predator, are we on the sidelines arguing about secondary theological issues while the house continues to burn? We have buckets full of living water, but how many have lost out on rescue from the Body of Christ because we are too busy pointing fingers at each other?

Conversations about theological issues remain important, so is there a way to accomplish our mission as believers in unity in spite of so many different perspectives? Caught in this tension, we need another signpost to follow.

Rupertus Meldenius's famous quote still rings true today: "In essentials unity, in nonessentials liberty, in all things charity." We don't have to agree on *everything* to murmurate and serve the world together! John Watson expands on this by saying that the unfortunate idea that unity is only possible in uniformity of doctrine "has been the poisoned spring of all dissensions that have torn Christ's body."[10] If you saw a burning home with people stuck inside, would you stop and survey the crowd outside on their doctrine before working with them to rescue those in peril? In the face of great need, we should be willing to work with others who are also willing to help save the orphan, the slave, the hungry, the poor, the spiritually lost, and the outcast even if our theology doesn't line up perfectly.

A note here: our aim with this signpost is not to aid the modern-day currents of relativism. If someone takes this signpost too far, it could have harmful unintended consequences. Just like when my children use a toy to hit their sibling. The toy was not designed for violence, but if used improperly, it can have devastating outcomes. The stark either/or of modernity and the deconstructionist approach to truth in postmodernity both leave us with some unanswered questions. There is a God who is the epicenter of all truth and He must remain the point of reference for us, but when we meet our maker, we will all find we were right about some things and wrong about others. As Scott Sauls says, "unless a human system is fully centered on God (no human system is), Jesus will have things to affirm and things to critique about it."[11] Our mission depends on our ability to show sacrificial love to one another and not on our ability to have every doctrine perfectly ironed out. God is okay with us being on a journey of learning and we should be too.

This is why sticking to core points of agreement as we work together does not diminish the importance of beliefs. Doctrines and traditions are important because they help the Church stay anchored, but in the same way that faith without works is dead, so doctrine without mission is dead.

Creeds such as the Nicene Creed and Apostle's Creed help us stick to common ground. Generations' worth of work has already been done to find core beliefs, and we would be foolish to ignore this tradition. The creeds fasten us to tradition and counterbalance today's cultural influences. It is so easy to become hyper-focused on our individual experiences and confuse a belief that is *cultural* with a belief that is *biblical*. When we approach believers who think differently than we do, being able to identify the difference between cultural interpretations and biblical absolutes is vital. Cultural values should not be given the same weight as biblical core values, because our opinion is worthless unless it lines up with Gospel truth. Research shows that diversity and unity initiatives are doomed to fail if we idolize the cultural values and identities we hold.[12] This means that speaking freely and comfortably about cultural assumptions should be seen as a valuable learning experience.

THE AUTHORITY OF SCRIPTURE

Many of the divisions within the Church stem from our diverse interpretations of Scripture. We rightly love Scripture, elevate it as the Word of God, and protect it against those who aim to devalue it. But what happens when our protection of it undermines the very mission the Scriptures call us to?

In his book *The Last Word*, N. T. Wright tackles the idea of the authority of Scripture. His goal is to help the Christian community navigate the Bible wars and many factions that arise from our spectrum of perspectives. For our conversation here, Wright's work can help expand our thinking and propel us toward unity even as we fulfill our desire to be faithful Bible-believing Christians.

Wright points out that diversity of interpretations is an endemic problem, found in many disciplines, when arriving at the understanding of an authoritative text—and we ought to

be "grown-up enough to cope with it."[13] For the Bible, we need
to see it within "the larger context which the biblical writers
themselves insist upon: that of the authority of God himself."[14]
The Bible is more than a devotional book, a tool for worship,
and more than a list of rules or a "convenient repository of
timeless truth"—it is all of those things but also much more.
Wright expands, saying:

> The risen Jesus, at the end of Matthew's gospel, does not
> say, "All authority in heaven and on earth is given to the
> books you are all going to write," but, "All authority in
> heaven and on earth is given to me." This ought to tell
> us, precisely if we are taking the Bible itself as seriously as
> we should, that we need to think carefully about what it
> might mean to think that the authority of Jesus is some-
> how exercised through the Bible.[15]

In other words, the Scriptures are all about Him, and His
authority and power are mediated *through* Scripture. Jesus
himself insisted on the authority of Scripture (Matthew 22,
Matthew 15, John 10:35) as He was the very fulfillment of the
law. He consciously brought "scripture to its long-awaited
climax."[16] **For Wright, saying that Scripture has authority is
really just a way of saying that when we read the Bible and
choose to live under it, we are willfully agreeing to live
under the Lordship of Jesus.**

So, what then is living under the sovereign Lordship of Jesus
all about? It certainly is not about filling our heads with right
answers. Since God's revelation is always to be understood in
the context of His mission, our faith is much more dynamic

than having a book on a shelf with all the right answers.[17] Living under his Lordship is first about believing in Christ, finding your identity in Him, and declaring Him Lord over your life, but it is also about declaring Him Lord over and above every kingdom of the world. Living under His reign means taking action toward His mission to heal the world. That is a more complicated and beautiful process than simply living under a sterile doctrine because it ties the authority of Scripture to our calling as believers.

So then, we are left with a better question: How does the authority and power of Scripture **serve** the purpose of growing Jesus' kingdom on earth as it is in heaven? Answering that question is much more interesting than settling theological disputes!

If you are not yet convinced, consider one more note: doctrines have meaning only in the context of a story. For followers of Christ, it is the story of a God who was separated from His creation and then set in motion a plan to be reunited with that creation. Heaven broke into our reality and Love itself endured a humiliating death on a cross as a guilt offering for sin to set creation free. Now those who through faith claim Him as Lord have a future promise of eternal fellowship with God and a vocational calling to make His kingdom come to life here and now as we wait for the return of the King. If we forget this entire story and approach the Bible only as a checklist of doctrines, we will continue to miss God's greater purposes and our true design. Wright puts it this way:

Jesus' resurrection has implications for our own personal resurrection, but if you read John 20, Luke 24, the early

church writers are talking a lot more about his Lordship, New Creation and the work before us rather than
a heavenly existence for the individual to avoid hell.
So why haven't we seen it? We really thought the only
story was "how do I get to heaven" and we've forced the
Gospel story into *that* story. It is possible to check all the
boxes doctrinally yet construct a different story and even
though you are trying to affirm them, you are actually
falsifying them outside the correct story. No Christian
tradition is exempt from this.[18]

May we be people who love the Word and follow it within
the right story! This is not easy work and Christians will continue to disagree on beliefs, but in the midst of that we can
focus on core beliefs and still work together rather than look for
the escape hatch. Having taken on the mind of Christ, may we
love one another in the context of *real* relationships, anchored
in history, tradition, and the Word.

As long as the Church of today continues to split and divide,
it will reinforce the narrative to the world that the Gospel is a
religion. Our faith is a marriage relationship with Christ, our
groom, but also a covenant relationship with our brothers and
sisters in Christ. Just as Hinlicky Wilson said, the "Church
turns divisive and ideological when it is severed from the gospel that brought it into being."[19] If we can spark a movement
toward unity, we will show that Jesus invites us into a much
richer adventure.

If we commit to dependence on the Holy Spirit through this
process, unity will never come at the sacrifice of truth, because
the Spirit will guide us in all truth (John 16:13) and we will

bear the fruits of love, joy, peace, and patience to lead as people of the new covenant.

A movement toward unity despite diversity of thought, belief, and preference is possible because unity does not mean uniformity. We offer these signposts to challenge the modern-day Church to incorporate *unity* into our definition of a *pure* church, to make strong statements instead of strong accusations, and to stick to the core values and beliefs as we labor together for the Lord.

In *Disunity in Christ*, Cleveland tells a story about a church in Kigali, Rwanda, that is offering the highest levels of relief to HIV/AIDS victims in that country, standing in the gap for spiritual and social change. What is incredible, Cleveland points out, is that "the church is composed of members of both the Hutus and Tutsis, two tribes that have a history of being arch-enemies, which climaxed in the genocide in 1994. Talk about overcoming hurdles in order to work together and bring about change."[20] Flying together and *murmurating* for the world to see *is* possible for the Church even in the face of chasms that seem too wide to bridge.

When we were yet *enemies* with God He still reached out to us. Following these signposts will feel like walking through mud at times, but if you dare walk this path with a clear vision of where God wants to take us, you will help unleash the mission of the Church like never before. The Scriptures are clear that any kingdom divided against itself will not stand (Luke 11:17). It is time to wake up and become the answer to Jesus' prayer—He prayed for it and He will also help us along the way. Let's make it a reality and not allow anything to get in the way.

Chapter 10

Principle 7: Contribution

If you try to satisfy yourself with a blessing from God, it will corrupt you.

—Oswald Chambers[1]

In research published by Anne Goodenough and her team in 2017, they studied data from over three thousand Murmurations. The data was submitted through citizen science collected over a two-year period that looked at size, duration, geography, habitats, and the temperature affecting Murmurations. They found the average duration of the Murmurations were twenty-six minutes, and the average size of Murmurations were noted to have 30,082 starlings, with the largest having up to 750,000!

In these unmatched formations, *every* bird contributes to the whole, and in so doing, each individual bird also benefits. Science shows that one of the main ways the individual starlings contribute is by transfer of information.[2] Every bird matters and has significance, because if one bird does not do its part, a missing link is created and information will not pass throughout the flock in time to avoid a predator.

Starlings also contribute by helping detect and spot the enemy. As Goodenough and her team explain, "Group anti-predator vigilance increases as the number of individuals in the group increases. This remains the case even when each individual in a group contributes less vigilance than a typical solitary individual."[3] In other words, even if each individual in the flock is *less* observant than normal, the collective vigilance exponentially increases their ability to spot their enemy. Mere contribution is a key component to the success of a Murmuration.

GIVE AND CONTRIBUTE GENEROUSLY

For believers, giving generously and sharing our resources is not only a small part of living a fruitful life, contribution is key in unleashing God's design for the Church. **When everyone contributes their strengths, gifts, and resources, the Church has the potential to become something distinctive, yet not formulaic.** This is what I believe Paul was talking about in 1 Corinthians 12 when he says:

> Just as a body, though one, has many parts, but all its many parts form one body, so it is with Christ. For we were all baptized by one Spirit so as to form one body—whether Jews or Gentiles, slave or free—and we were all given the one Spirit to drink. Even so the body is not made up of one part but of many.
>
> 1 Corinthians 12:12–14 NIV

For Paul, the gifts and talents God bestows to each individual are not for their own gain, but rather for the common good and edification of the Church (1 Corinthians 14). It is a gift that God expects you to immediately re-gift. Oswald Chambers's words echo this truth: "If you are always keeping blessings to yourself and never learning to pour out anything 'to the Lord,' other people will never have their vision of God expanded through you."[4] We are designed to contribute and bring our God-given gifts to the table. With a view of the larger system at play, we will learn to see how we are a part of the interplay between ministries, churches, and individual believers in our community.

CONTRIBUTION ON STEROIDS

Something incredible happens every day in Mumbai, India: lunches are delivered.

Not impressed yet? The truly amazing part is *how* the lunches are delivered: each day in Mumbai, there is a large team of *dabbawalas*, or lunch box men, that put on a logistics clinic. They expertly execute a lunch delivery system with enough efficiency and finesse to make FedEx jealous.

It all began 125 years ago when a businessman who worked in the downtown corporate district wanted to have a home-cooked meal for lunch. He hired the first dabbawala to deliver him lunch, and it quickly caught on. Demand soared from other businessmen wanting a home-cooked meal, and a huge business evolved. Today, there are five thousand employed dabbawalas who deliver two hundred thousand meals daily!

Dabbawala loading his bike (henktennapel—stock.adobe.com)

Lunch pails prepped for delivery (henktennapel—stock.adobe.com)

Okay, this is the part you will hardly believe. Are you sitting down?

Only one in six million lunch deliveries is ever late!

Every one of the two hundred thousand daily meals comes from the suburbs, made in the private homes of a network of cooks called *mommas*. The day for a dabbawala begins by visiting their route of homes and picking up the prepared lunch boxes from the mommas. This requires going up and down flights of stairs in many buildings. They then each carry thirty to forty lunch boxes through traffic, mud, and bad roads to make the deliveries—even in the monsoon season. At train stations they meet up with other team members, and each dabbawala follows a special coding system to sort all the lunches to send them on their various routes. In just a four-hour time period, between 9:00 a.m. and 1:00 p.m., two hundred thousand lunches are picked up, sorted, and then delivered throughout Mumbai. After the delivery is completed, the dabbawalas gather together to pray and have their own lunch, building relationships around their strategy.

Cool, right? Well, the job is only half done at that point. The dabbawalas will then go through the entire process again *backward*, collecting the empty lunch boxes and returning them to the suburban homes where they will be cleaned and filled again for the next day.

They do this with no IT infrastructure and 85 percent illiteracy among dabbawalas. Simply incredible! So how can they accomplish such superhuman execution?

Everyone contributes.

They do this through a deep culture of interdependence, pride in their work, and an unstoppable drive to accomplish their common mission. Pedestrians even make way for the lunch box men because they know dabbawalas don't stop for anyone. They realize they each play a critical role in their larger strategy.

Recall our Relationships and Strategy graph. Day after day, these lunch box deliverymen display a nearly perfect picture of the power of common strategy as an outgrowth of healthy relationships. Their own website states that "teamwork and trust is what makes a common Dabbawala do extraordinary things."[5] Paul Goodman from Carnegie Mellon studied their amazing system and he points out that the dabbawalas have an adaptive human system, but it is based on strict rules and roles.[6] Sounds a bit like a Murmuration, doesn't it?

It is an adaptive system where individuals follow strict behavioral rules—influencing *and* being influenced by those around them. How can such a system remain agile and adaptive yet also extremely effective? Everyone knows their role and contributes.

ONE PLUS ONE IS MORE THAN TWO IN THE KINGDOM OF GOD

In the Lord's economy, we can give generously with no concern for how it will affect us. We bring our offering to the household of God and allow Him to multiply the gifts. Contribution is all about knowing that we matter and that we have something to offer. It is not only about sharing financial and physical resources, it is also about sharing our heritage, cultures, and perspectives. Without cultural, gender, and ethnic diversity, we actually have an incomplete perspective of God.[7]

Think of it this way: **when we bring our diversity to the table, we can actually contribute to one another's understanding of God!** All sorts of beautiful things

When we bring our diversity to the table, we can actually contribute to one another's understanding of God!

can happen when we contribute to the kingdom. That is precisely what happened to Mike and a group of leaders reaching students:

MIKE'S STORY

A number of years ago I was meeting with leaders at the Urban Youth Workers Institute (UYWI) to dream about how we could work better together. Since most youth ministry is done by bi-vocational leaders, we wanted to learn what it would look like to network diverse leaders together.

After leaving the meeting, I committed to meet monthly with one particular leader to know him better. We were from different backgrounds, but we talked about our families and ministries and began to dream about what it might look like to work together. After a whole year of building relationship, I asked him to help me facilitate a networking meeting that I had been leading for a number of years. He brought his friends and I brought mine. The result was interesting and challenging all at the same time. We realized even though we may have had different ideas of how to do ministry and reach others for Christ, we all had something valuable to contribute that would not only multiply our efforts but also enrich the experience of serving together.

Before working with UYWI, a group of youth leaders in Southern California had a vision to equip and empower students to make a difference on their campuses, and so we led a conference called Turn Your Campus. The leaders represented local churches and para-church ministries of all types: Youth for Christ, National Network of Youth Ministries, Christian Educators Association, Biola University, and many local churches. For fifteen years, through general sessions and over fifty workshops, we were reaching about five hundred students.

After years with the same results for the Turn Your Campus event, we decided we needed to make some changes. That's when we invited our friends from UYWI to help produce our opening session. They invited their friends, and things immediately began to sound and look different. The worship was amazing, led by an ethnically diverse band. They took worship to a new level of excitement and participation. It didn't take long for the look of the audience to change, too, and soon the room was filled with such diverse people, I imagine it is what heaven looks like. The outreach event more than doubled—and now we have grown to more than seventeen hundred students and their leaders!

It's amazing what can happen when you give ministry away and don't care who gets the credit. Seeing unity unfold before your eyes is worth it. We really can make each other better when we contribute and bring our strengths to the table.

ADDING VALUE

Do you want to contribute your strengths? Try this paradigm shift: add value to others. How often do you get a phone call from someone simply asking if they can help with something? Most of the calls we get are from people who need something *from* us. What if we flipped the script and began seeing our relationships as opportunities to contribute and give something away?

In *Never Eat Alone*, Keith Ferazzi shares how this perspective is what helped him experience such great professional success. He quickly rose to become the CMO of the consulting firm Deloitte and then CMO for Starwood Hotels at thirty-two, making him the youngest CMO for a Fortune 500 company at the time. In his bestselling book, he talks about finding ways to bring value to others, because when we give of our time and expertise generously, everyone ends up winning in the end.[8]

The kingdom principle is to not think in terms of what others can give you, but rather find ways to use our God-given gifts to contribute and bring value to other people's lives.

This movement will cost us something. In fact, if living Christ's vision for unity is not hard, then we are not doing it right! But we should not let that hinder us. In the long run, like the starlings, we will get back so much more in return. The work toward unity will require sacrifice, but take heart because we get to be like Christ in the process: His ministry was incarnational and came at great personal cost. He gave *everything* that He had, and now we get the privilege of doing the same. Along the way, just remember to avoid the temptation to get recognized for your contribution. Our contributions must be offerings poured out for the Lord and not for our gain.

We each have a responsibility to contribute to the growth of unity in the Church and also to the greater collective missional work of the Church. You are holding a piece of the puzzle, and Christ's design will not be complete without your contribution!

Part Three

PRACTICAL STEPS TO HELP SPARK A MURMURATION MOVEMENT

In part 1, we established God's design for unity and our current reality of division as the Church. This hopefully generated the creative tension and urgency we need for unity among followers of Jesus to explode.

In part 2, we dove into the Murmuration, learning about the phenomena and drawing out principles that we can follow to unleash collective movement in the Body of Christ.

Now, in this final section it's time to learn how to move our fragmented Church toward God's design! We want to give you just a few lessons learned from over forty years of combined ministry and networking experiences, to help you embrace the vision and move forward with passion!

Chapter 11

Radical Optimism

Now to him who is able to do far more abundantly than
all that we ask or think, according to the power at work
within us, to him be glory in the church and in Christ
Jesus throughout all generations, forever and ever. Amen.
—Ephesians 3:20–21 ESV

By now, you may be thinking, *This is a nice message, but it's
naive. There are two thousand years of negative church history,
and I can share personal modern-day stories to show that unity is
impossible.*

Admittedly, our stark reality is overwhelming and can produce doubt. We spend so much time, money, and energy to fight
for peace, justice, and love, yet unity continually eludes us. We
spend billions of dollars to establish entire governments that
create laws toward attaining harmony. We want to diminish
violence, crime, divorce, and cry out for racial reconciliation,
unity, and of course the ever-elusive "reach across the aisle." Yet
unity remains a voice continually around the next corner.

This frustrating reality leaves us with a big question: Is the unity Jesus prayed for in John 17 really attainable, or is it just false hope? Truth be told, we can have all the relationships, strategy, and principles to follow, but if we do not first believe deep in our bones that unity is possible through the power of God, the movement will fall flat.

Before we go any further, we need to fill our tanks with *radical optimism*.[1] It is the fuel that will propel the vision when things get difficult. This was the same sort of optimism that fueled Martin Luther King Jr. in the face of civil rights injustices. It was this same sort of optimism that set William Wilberforce ablaze to overturn the slave trade in England, and it was this perspective that permeated Nelson Mandela's spirit to bring about the anti-apartheid revolution in South Africa. These legends faced mountains, yet they knew change was possible!

So our vision of massive proportions, or our *BHAG* (big hairy audacious goal)[2] for the Jim Collins fans, is this: the same unity that exists between Father, Son, and Holy Spirit is actually possible in the Church today. Well, it's not actually our vision—as the master reconciler, it's God's dream and design, but He has made each of us a major player in the equation. If we can keep this optimism, we have a chance at filling our roles in the Body as He intended. So how can we stay radically optimistic? Three quick ideas:

1. Remember, unity is God's design
2. Let faith arise
3. Celebrate short-term wins and tell stories of unity

REMEMBER, UNITY IS GOD'S DESIGN

We find great hope when our eyes turn to God and the divine family: the only sphere that perfectly represents unity in all its forms. God's very essence of unity within diversity is engrained in the design of creation and the Church. Here we see that unity already exists perfectly, unity is *His* desire, and we are invited into it.

One of the fascinating things about the intimacy in the Trinity is that it connotes the intimacy unique to a family. In this Holy Family, Jesus shows His perfect submission to the Father and yet clearly states that they are so deeply united that when you get to know one, you automatically know the other. They defer glory to each other and show that submission is a holy act! The Father speaks of His blessing and favor on the Son (Matthew 3:17). The Son, even in His moment of deepest prayer and anguish, when facing the pain and suffering of the cross, still was submissive to the will of the Father (Luke 22:42). Also, while Jesus walked the earth, He not only pointed to the Father, but also to the One who is to come, the Holy Spirit (John 14). They are eternally patient, forgiving, of one purpose, and full of faith, hope, love, and justice. Everything we crave is represented in the God Sphere.

When we look at our world, we find that there are many "families" at play too. Every day, we move in and out of these different families or "spheres" through an interconnectedness in the system of families. In other words, our world as we know it is in a constant dance or a sort of Murmuration—a truly universal and cosmic interconnectedness between our spheres.

So is unity false hope in our spheres? No! Jesus confidently asked His Father for unity, because He knew that through His work on the cross, we could enter in the community of the Trinity. He actually believes that the Church can become one unified body, an indivisible, interwoven, submissive, intimate, moving, dancing, and murmurating body, working for God's kingdom.

You may be thinking: "Yeah, but the unity Christ prayed for is not possible today and is for the ultimate second coming of Christ." My response to that is simple and rooted in *why* Jesus wants the body to be one. Jesus prayed for unity so that the world will know He is Lord! This *why* would make no sense after Christ returns because everyone will clearly know on that day and every knee will bow (Romans 14:11, Philippians 2:10). If God wants to use the unity of the Church as a means of showing the world His awesome love and restorative power, it doesn't fit for that to be something that is saved just for a quick snapshot at the end of time for all to see.

This road toward unity will require lionhearted radical optimism, but if we are to learn how to fly together, we must remember this is God's plan.

LET FAITH ARISE

Try this experiment. Read the following statement out loud: "Today, the global evangelical Church, in all dimensions, can become unified as one body exactly the way it was designed to be."

What was your internal reaction to that statement? I'd bet your inner voice immediately shot that statement out of the sky. "No way is that possible." The vast majority of readers will read that line and have a negative internal reaction. Truth be told, I have to fight that negative reaction in my own heart. This is heavy stuff. This is why radical optimism is a discipline we must learn and continually reaffirm in one another. The way we fight cynicism about unity is through radical optimism produced by faith in the power of God. Just like light always beats darkness, faith *always* beats cynicism.

The negative power of cynicism can be looming, defeating us before the battle even begins. Knowing that humans have a tendency toward cynicism is important, but identifying the *source of our individual cynicism* gives us even more power over this massive form of resistance to unity.[3] What are some of the things you have experienced that contribute to the resistance? What might be beneath the surface of your heart that might contribute to cynicism? Unearthing these through self-evaluation and contemplation is a wonderful exercise to make way for faith to fill our hearts!

While writing this on sabbatical in California, there were some serious wildfires in the Pacific Northwest. The combination of drought and heat creates prime opportunities for these devastating fires to erupt. To stop these fires, one of the main strategies firefighters employ is to dig "fire lines"—which is basically digging a trough, sometimes up to three feet wide, so that the fire cannot continue to spread. The reason this strategy works to contain the fire is because it is a "break in fuel" and removes all of the flammable material on the surface. The

U.S. National Parks Service explains it this way: "Once the fire is 'contained,' the hard, dirty work of mop up goes into full swing to bring the fire under control. Each ember will be painstakingly sought and put out. The entire fire perimeter, and sometimes the entire fire area, is felt with bare hands (cold trailed) to be sure there is no longer any heat left to allow the fire to escape."[4]

If radical optimism is the fuel for our unity movement, then cynicism is the fire line that stops the spread of the vision. The movement wants to spread like wildfire, but the enemy is relentlessly digging these lines between us, planting cynicism, and quickly the embers cool off. Think about the dedication of the firefighters to feel the entire fire area by hand! We must realize that this is the sort of ferocious determination that the enemy has to ensure that this fire of unity does not break free. The united people of God would be the most devastating blow to his purposes.

Faith, on the other hand, is fuel to the fire. We serve a God with immeasurable power, and He sits enthroned above the entire universe with the earth as His footstool—what can't He do?! With a clear picture of who we serve and what He wants, our job is to open our hearts and let faith flood in. Our faith *can* move mountains. We are each an ember that lasts but a minute. But when combined with others, we can create a Murmuration of embers that will set a fire that blazes to the heavens!

Where did the category-smashing and earth-shaking believers go? Have we just become cynical to the power of God and comfortable in our small flocks? Where are the titans of faith like those described in Hebrews:

And what more shall I say? For time would fail me to tell of Gideon, Barak, Samson, Jephthah, of David and Samuel and the prophets—who through faith conquered kingdoms, enforced justice, obtained promises, stopped the mouths of lions, quenched the power of fire, escaped the edge of the sword, were made strong out of weakness, became mighty in war, put foreign armies to flight. Women received back their dead by resurrection. Some were tortured, refusing to accept release, so that they might rise again to a better life. Others suffered mocking and flogging, and even chains and imprisonment. They were stoned, they were sawn in two, they were killed with the sword.

Hebrews 11:32–37 ESV

Let faith arise! May we resolve to believe down in our bones in God's design. It's more than just knowing God's vision in our minds; it is a fire in our guts that sets us ablaze, with a willingness to lay our lives down for the Kingdom!

CELEBRATE SHORT-TERM WINS AND TELL STORIES OF UNITY

The art of celebration is sometimes lost in our culture. One of the things I love about Hebrew culture is how seriously they take their celebrations, coming-of-age ceremonies, feasts, and holidays. Mostly, holidays in our Western culture mean a day off from school or work and typically do not carry the same weight and significance.

To sustain radical optimism on the road toward unity, learning the art of celebration will be critical. John Kotter, professor emeritus at Harvard Business School, calls this *celebrating short-term wins*. He defines a short-term win as a significant positive event or improvement that happens within eighteen months or less.[5] These positive events must be celebrated, talked about at the water cooler, sent out via broadcast email, or even taped to the back of the bathroom stall doors. We must become the most captivating and inventive storytellers. To anchor any changes in an organization, success stories must be commended and clearly visible to everyone.

Passion for unity in the Church will quickly become wishful thinking if the chemistry of the movement is not infused with the ability to celebrate short-term wins. This is powerful because these celebrations accumulate over time and snowball into real results.

In his recent book *Shoe Dog*, Phil Knight tells the amazing journey of building Nike into a multinational company. He recounts how by 1979, Nike had a huge headquarters, was sponsoring major celebrity talent, and on track to hit sales of $140 million. Yet, Knight recalls that just like the new minimalist decor in his office, he felt utterly empty. Instead of being able to enjoy how far he'd come, he could only see how far he had to go. Then, with profound wisdom and perspective, he shares, "When you see only problems, you're not seeing clearly."[6] Despite the massive success he enjoyed, he had a hard time celebrating the short-term wins.

One way we celebrate short-term wins is by storytelling. We need to develop the nets to capture stories of unity in the

Church and then the channels through which those stories can be shared publicly. If we move progressively toward the vision but do so in silence, the movement will lose momentum. We have attempted to create just one of these spaces to capture and share these stories. Our website www.DesignedForMore Book.com connects you to a platform for telling positive stories about how the Church is moving toward completion as we implement the *Murmuration* vision. Go check it out now to read other stories and share your own!

The biblical message is clear and direct: Jesus wants the oneness of believers to be a reality, today. The bottom line is that we will either believe this or not. If you believe and have the daring determination that this journey will require, then resolve to be filled with faith that God can do it! Also resolve to not only cultivate radical optimism in yourself, but also help others stay optimistic and spur others on to greater faith (Hebrews 10:24–25). Even if this road is hard or makes us uncomfortable, stay optimistic and keep the course. Just because the road is hard does not let us off the hook. Woe to us if we are not willing to become uncomfortable to fight for God's vision and design!

To those that might still doubt this is possible, I ask: Is the cross such a small thing, that there is still more God needs to do? Jesus said it is finished and there is no "bigger" thing that we need to wait for—His work is complete and we can be too. We don't have to wait for a distant day in the future. Christ has already done everything that needs to be done. As believers in Christ, we are already united into something so much larger than ourselves. Let's make it tangible for the world to see.

Imagine the Church engaging, as one, to solve social problems, transforming entire school systems, reducing poverty, providing clean blood and water, undertaking global economic development and food distribution, fighting for justice while sharing the Gospel and creating disciples all the while. The world will look in awe and see the glory of God as the Spirit conducts our Murmurations.

Chapter 12

Creating the MO

Our separate, isolated efforts will not stop the flood of increasing evil in our cities if we, as Christ's church, remain isolated from each other.

—Francis Frangipane[1]

God's design for unity is not simply for unity's sake. In the same way that our body makes blood for a greater purpose, our unity is the lifeblood that propels the mission of our Church body forward. The whole point of unity and sparking Murmurations is to build the Kingdom of God through united, citywide strategies for our communities to experience the lordship of Christ. Just like the Murmuration, the secret to our power is what we become when we come together in Christ.

Are we strategic in how we currently reach our city and the world? Communities typically have many churches or ministries, all doing outreach work, but is there a collective plan for working together for a broader impact? We can't do everything together, but what *are* we going to do together? This chapter is all about getting our communities to think in terms of collective impact and the power behind united efforts.

So how do we get things going? What is the process for unity to come to life in the Church? It all begins with the "MO": the sequence of events that must occur for unity to get to a tipping point. The flow looks like this: MOments + MOmentum = MOvement.

We must create **MOments** for individuals that build **MOmentum,** which grows into a **MOvement.** In our experience, any serious work toward unity begins with individuals having a specific moment when God reveals the imperative nature of unity. Then that individual shares the vision with others, creating momentum. Finally, if enough momentum is built *for a sustained period of time*, the momentum transitions into something almost entirely new: a movement!

We've seen this happen in other communities and the outcomes are powerful.

MIKE'S STORY

One of my favorite examples of creating the MO is the story behind "See You at the Pole" (SYATP). It is an awesome story of a "God idea" that was owned by a denomination but was given away. You may know SYATP as a widespread movement when students gather at their school flagpole on a specific morning to pray for their campus.

I was in the meeting in 1990 when I watched the leadership of the Southern Baptists share the idea for the first time. They had an event that took place in Texas and Oklahoma where students gathered for a weekend retreat. After this conference, they decided to close out the weekend by going down to the local high school to pray. They gathered around the flagpole, and a national prayer movement was born. As the Baptist leaders shared the story of what occurred in Oklahoma and Texas, their enthusiasm was contagious. You could sense that something was about to happen.

Instead of wanting to own and control this idea, I watched these leaders give it away and create momentum by inviting others to the table. The result has been an international movement. The National Network of Youth Ministries (NNYM) and Student Discipleship Ministries took on the challenge to partner and used their broad reach to spread the word—the rest is history. Over the years, literally millions of students worldwide have gathered around their flagpoles to pray for their campuses. To this day, students still gather at their flagpoles, praying for their schools. I'm so grateful to the Southern Baptist leaders who had a "God Idea" and gave it away so it could be multiplied many times over. A MOment for a few students and leaders grew into MOmentum when the leaders chose to invite others into the vision. Through unity, it exploded into a worldwide MOvement!

MOMENT

The work of unity is the work of God, which begins in each individual's heart. Although unity conversations tend to focus on the group collective, there is an intensely personal aspect to the work of unity. Mainly because it means we each must become more like Christ. The ultimate result of unity is outward mission, but only as an outcome of what God has already done in the spirit of each person. A Murmuration in the Church must then begin from the inside out at the individual level. That is ground zero.

As we explored earlier, Greek language has two words for "time": *kairos* and *kronos*. *Kronos* refers to sequential time and chronological order of events. *Kairos*, however, refers to a critical or singular point in time, a MOment. In relationship to spiritual growth, *kairos* means "the opportune time of God" and the intervention of God into human history. In this context, the singular point is the intervention of God. We cannot plan it; the decision belongs to God.

My *kairos* moment was the experience with the Fusion events; for Mike, it was hearing the unity message at Promise Keepers and his work with the Overtime events in San Diego. These moments are decisive experiences that change everything.

What is your *kairos* MOment when God expanded your vision to His design? If you are still waiting for a moment to capture the massive vision for unity, invite the Lord *right now* to give you a MOment! If you have already had a *kairos* moment, ask the Lord to give you opportunities to help others experience the same moment so we can generate MOmentum!

MOMENTUM

When enough individuals have moments that change their perspective to see God's ultimate design for the Church, momentum begins to build. At this point, however, the next steps are critical. Individual moments don't always turn into real traction or momentum for unity in a community. The work is so big and challenging that it's easy to get distracted or hope someone else steps up. Our *kairos* moments are powerful, but their impact can only have lasting results in our lives if they are fueled and propelled by others around us.

One easy way individuals can turn MOments into MOmentum is to *share* their experience with others. Talking more regularly about unity through blogs, on social media, in sermons, or over coffee builds momentum. This is how we can raise awareness about the imperative nature of unity and also be reminded that we are not alone in the work. You can easily do this in the context of your Seven Influential Neighbors, a network meeting, or within a small group at your church.

MIKE'S STORY

In my twenty-two years of working with local networks, I have seen that most of our gatherings are either relationally driven or event driven. Networks that are too far on either end of the spectrum eventually die, or at the least have minimal impact. This type of networking gives people a good reason to not show up and commit to the group. Time is valuable and we don't need another meeting, especially if it is poorly run. We need relationships and strategy in balance.

It's easy to settle into what is comfortable. It's even easier to stay in our echo chamber, going deeper with those closest to us, and think we "have unity." I have seen networks meet consistently for years and accomplish no more than build deeper relationship with each other.

I'm dreaming and praying for the day when a relationally strong group becomes intentional and strategic in building momentum for their cities. I'm dreaming of a critical mass of leaders who come together and say, "It's time. We are at war and have no other option but to stand together, united."

What does it look like to build a faith community that goes outside organizational lines to move forward in purpose and mission, creating "momentum" for your city?

Building MOmentum for a network starts with gathering people from different sections of the community. Many times, we just flat out leave the table too soon. We need to stay at the table long enough to really hear what God is saying and create conversations that speak to both the personal and professional lives of those involved. These meetings should also resource people and give them a reason to be committed and stay. This means incorporating a process of communicating and planning.

We have become stagnant and safe. It's time for our networks to be dangerous. By asking, *"What can we do together that we could not do separately?"* we can be stretched out of our comfort zones, calling each other to MOmentum for thoughtful citywide planning. Creating momentum is not rocket science, but we must be creative, purposeful, and calculated in our planning to impact our cities, nation, and the world.

Paul Fleischmann, in his book *Better Together*, challenges leaders to have a clear strategy. He asks: **"Do you have a plan for cooperation that is measurable?"**[2] You can have a common purpose, relationships, and credible leadership, but without a clear and measurable strategy for getting there, little momentum will be built. And since Jesus gave believers the Holy Spirit as our guide (John 14), we can have confidence that He will lead us to a plan that will yield supernatural results. Imagine the Holy Spirit over your city. What needs would He see in your community? What resources would He see? In light of those things, how would the Spirit use the diverse parts of the Church to serve your community?

Don't be intimidated by the size of the task. Ultimately, our work should happen because we're being obedient to the promptings of God's "still small voice" (1 Kings 19:12 KJV). Yes, it will take work to build the "MO" for a city, but "waiting to start until you have everything in place is usually a recipe for achieving nothing."[3] What if we drove across town and bought someone coffee or lunch and shared our stories? What if we really began to know and trust those Seven Influential Neighbors? It's time to come to the table and stay long enough to know and trust one another. Let's discern together the heart of God for our cities and make such a splash that city officials call us because they realize we have something to offer. When individual passion for unity becomes visible through united outreach efforts with other believers, we are moving from MOmentum to MOvement!

MOVEMENT

If we keep meeting as we are, we will keep getting what we've got. But imagine if we changed things up. Imagine if a critical mass of people had God-inspired MOments, then sustained MOmentum with other believers to spark a *MOvement*!

Like the Murmuration, the end result will be an intentional alignment of citywide strategies. Like expert musicians playing together, we will be an orchestra playing as unto the Lord, and for the world to experience the beauty. We have yet to experience fully this mode of operating as the Body of Christ. Consider also that moving toward unity, like the first falling domino, also starts all sorts of other movements like See You at the Pole!

One way to view this is to imagine that Paul's exhortation in 1 Corinthians on spiritual gifts not only applies to individuals, but also to ministries and churches. Is it possible that each church has its own spiritual gifts because of the makeup of the individuals in that particular fellowship? Is it possible that God has filled particular faith communities with, let's say for example, a high concentration of people with compassion or generosity so that they focus on reaching the poor in a city? Maybe in that same community, another church has a concentration of members with the gift of leadership. God may have placed them in that community to be an influence in the political and social infrastructures. We need to start seeing our place in the larger body and what we have to contribute. The key is knowing what part you have been given and what your role is for the function of the body.

We are calling for grassroots, organic, local, and united

initiatives. The top-down work of the ecumenical movement must continue, but we need a groundswell to mobilize and meet those high-level conversations in the middle.

We want local and regional Murmurations, but a brief warning about over-contextualizing the movement. We must maintain a local focus yet keep a global and historical perspective of the Church. The danger is to become too radically contextual to our cultures and *only* use our local concepts and framework for Christian teaching and worship. We do not want to split our faith from accountability and the powerful heritage it carries. The Christian movement was birthed in the crosshairs of Judaism and Hellenism and has a long heritage outside of those contexts too. The challenge of the first disciples was to communicate the message of Christ in such a way that it was culturally contextualized without diluting and distorting the message.[4] Our challenge is the same today.

Our hope rests on individuals experiencing a *moment* that leads to *momentum*, which eventually sparks a *movement*. There will always be problems, conflict, setbacks, and bumps along the way. But for every one of us, our task is to generate enough momentum so we can get over the speed bumps when they come. Our churches and cities are waiting for leaders who will champion the cause of unity, and intentionally and strategically pray and plan to build the "MO." This is the only way we can get a unity movement to Gladwell's famous *tipping point*.[5]

So how can you help spark a movement? Start by allowing God to show you His design, watch momentum build as you share it with others, and then wait for the Spirit to unleash the Murmuration movement!

Chapter 13

Rules to Live By

We believe our future security and prosperity depends on our collective ability to act "as one."

—Baghai and Quigley[1]

God designed unity to be the highway through which His followers could lead a radical kingdom building force. As we begin to operate within our design and practice the Murmuration principles, we will need a few guiding rules for the journey that will act as guardrails to protect our momentum.

No matter the position, title, status, or authority you might hold, the following rules to live by are urgently vital. They apply to everyone and we must remember to not only operate by them, but also use our influence to help others do the same. To be the united Body of Christ, our journey will require us to

- engage in strategic prayer and dependence on the Holy Spirit.

- keep it simple. Remember, small changes can produce high leverage results.
- remember that our greatest power lies in removing limiting factors.

ENGAGE IN STRATEGIC PRAYER AND DEPEND ON THE HOLY SPIRIT

The fight for unity is not a "fix it overnight" process. Any meaningful movement toward unity that is to last must be immersed in faith, prayer, and daily dependence on the Spirit. Unity will require time in prayer and total dependence on God. We cannot forget for one minute that God is the source of unity and it is only through *Him* that we have any chance at all of success. Human endeavors have the tendency to produce static organizational structures that beg for life. Through the habit of prayer and dependence on the Holy Spirit we are reminded to always give God the space to bring life into our structure. This also recalibrates our perspective to see beyond our circumstances when things get difficult.

> Any meaningful movement toward unity that is to last must be immersed in faith, prayer, and daily dependence on the Spirit.

In Genesis 11, we find the intriguing story of Babel, when man united through their common language to accomplish great things. They wanted to build a tower to reach the heavens and become like God. Because their purposes and desires were focused on the wrong priorities and objectives, however, their unity actually became dangerous. Consequently, God divided them into many people with different languages.

The story of Babel highlights the destructive power of unity if not guided by the Holy Spirit or used for the wrong goal. We still fall into the trap of trusting man's strength so quickly. Prayer and dependence on the Spirit become daily reminders that our work is done in and through God's power alone. This is not a ritualistic obligation. Like a doctor resetting a broken arm, prayer is a powerful force that reestablishes the supremacy of God's will in our lives and in our communities. In the end, we are set free from worry as we trust that He is in control.

Fast-forward to Acts 2 and we find the beautiful redemption of the tower of Babel story from Genesis 11. As the early Church was in fellowship and prayer together, a mighty rushing wind filled the entire place and tongues of fire rested on each of them as they began to speak different tongues. What God had once split in the ancient story, He was now bringing back together, not with a traditional language, but with the central language of love. This new universal language supersedes all previous kingdoms and brings unity again to humanity, but a unity with the right priorities and centrally focused on God.

Pentecost itself was a sign to the Apostles of the breaking down of barriers. The first, most evident barrier was that of language, as they freely communicated with foreigners in their native tongues. The diversity of the crowd is clear from the variety of languages and cultures (Acts 2:6–8, 9–11). Luke is laying the groundwork that this was an initial softening for the proclamation of the Gospel to Jew and Gentile alike—this new gift of the Holy Spirit was for *every* nation and *every* person.

With access to such power, we must use it to propel unity and our work as believers. It is in moments of prayer that God realigns our priorities, reminds us of His dreams and His design, and sets us on track. There is an important personal dynamic to prayer because in this realignment, cynicism, division, and bitterness are redefined and we become more self-aware. We learn who we are, know more of God, and are reminded that we are not Him!

Our personal prayer life not only reorganizes our interior selves, but prayer is also a powerful corporate unifying tool. Paul Fleischmann, president emeritus of the National Network of Youth Ministries, points out that simply waiting on the Lord together is an act of unity.[2] As we begin to live into the Murmuration principles and have growing relationships and strategies with our neighbors, the trajectory of our impact will exponentially explode if we come together and pray first.

This is the magnificent picture given to us in Acts, when the early believers gathered to pray: "These all continued with one accord in prayer and supplication, with the women, and Mary the mother of Jesus, and with his brethren" (Acts 1:14 KJV).

The original Greek text for this phrase "in one accord" is *homothymadon*, which is a compound word meaning "to rush along in unison."[3] It is used over eleven times in the book of Acts alone. The original word connotes imagery of a musical orchestra or chorus in prayer. With many different and diverse notes sounding together yet harmonizing under the leadership of the Holy Spirit, this is the beautiful *homothymadon, or Murmuration,* that the early Church was enjoying.

It is time that our prayers change. Let's stop telling God how big our dividing walls are and start telling our walls how big our God is. Matthew 7:7 says that if we knock, the door will be opened. I believe that we have been knocking on some wrong doors. With radical optimism, let's knock on the doors of heaven for unity to spread like wildfire in the Church. I echo John Piper's words: "So let it not be said of us: 'You do not have, because you do not ask' (James 4:2)...But know this. God also loves to give breakthroughs in the twinkling of an eye."[4] Let's pray with faith, knowing God can do in one day what we think would take one hundred years—let's ask Him to move mightily!

We cannot overstate how central dependence on the Holy Spirit and prayer are to unleashing Christ's vision for unity. This is where true power rests to overcome the sin and human weakness that keeps us divided. Jesus prayed His radical prayer for us because it is attainable through the help of the Holy Spirit, who produces life-giving fruit on individual, local, and global levels (Galatians 5).

KEEP IT SIMPLE. REMEMBER, SMALL CHANGES CAN PRODUCE HIGH LEVERAGE RESULTS

Small changes can have huge results.[5] In the end, the most powerful things that propel unity are actually quite simple. We don't need marketing budgets of global proportions, a famous charismatic leader, or a massive control center to become the united Church Christ wants us to be. We can begin to murmurate with our seven churches, individuals, or ministries and the movement will grow quickly. Just like in the Murmuration, local interactions have the potential to generate global order!

If we resolve to pursue Christ's vision for unity with unrelenting passion, we will need to know *which* small changes have power to produce leverage. According to systems thinking, leverage is a change that requires minimum effort but produces significant and lasting improvement. The Church is a huge system with over two billion professing Christians in the world,[6] so applying leverage correctly to such a complex and interlacing assembly is hard. Course correction is possible, however. Like the rudder on a ship, or a bridle on a horse, small well-placed solutions will produce incredible results.

The discipline of systems thinking helps us see which small changes have power. Finding the leverage we need to become a *whole* church lies in our ability to first see things in *wholes*. Only when we learn to see the bigger system at play can we identify the small things that can produce significant results. (By the way, this is another reason to be radically optimistic— our movement toward unity will require minimum effort with the right leverage!)

So how do we find this elusive leverage toward unity and the Church's mission? We press in to systems thinking. Usually, we will find the highest leverage in small fulcrums.

One of the easiest ways to learn systems thinking is to know God. He is the master systems thinker and ultimate definition of unity within diversity. How can God simultaneously work all things together for the good of those who love Him (Romans 8:28)? His perspective is unlimited; the more we know Him and learn His ways, the more we will see things the way He does.

A second way we can practically learn the new discipline is to use the "5 WHYs" tool, also called the *Why-Why Chart*.[7] This is a "root cause analysis" tool that helps us stop addressing symptoms and focus on the source of our problems. The basic concept is that by asking "why" you will usually arrive at the root cause of a problem within five or less "whys." Each time you answer the "why" question, it takes you a level deeper and teaches you to see the system. For example:

Starting issue: We have dissatisfied customers.

1st Why? Customers are not getting their products on time.
2nd Why? We have poor communication between the sales and shipping departments.
3rd Why? We hire team members too quickly without proper training on our system.
4th Why? We have too many projects going on.
5th Why? We have prioritized profit over people.

Our tendency is to want quick and easy solutions; however, that only results in reacting to events and circumstances. We must resist this reflex because reactionary thinking reduces our ability to think and act systemically. It is a journey. As Salter McNeil puts it, "Transformation is rarely linear. It's usually more of a winding process."[8] Learning a new discipline and committing to the process will give us the ability to see which small changes hold the power.

Working toward unity is a daunting task, but we can all do something small. Begin a new relationship. Identify a limited achievable objective with your Seven Influential Neighbors.[9] Pray. Give something away without worrying about getting credit. Invite someone to coffee. Live the Murmuration principles. Start somewhere. Eventually your small changes will reach a tipping point and become much more together.

REMEMBER THAT OUR GREATEST POWER LIES IN REMOVING LIMITING FACTORS

Small changes can produce high leverage results, but the *greatest* leverage lies in removing the thing that holds us back. Most of the time in human endeavors, we work toward our vision or goals by focusing on *adding* work, new programs, or initiatives. We invoke bigger budgets, more phone calls, or marketing to push growth. We spend most of our time working to climb *over* the boulder in our own way instead of moving the boulder.

In systems thinking lingo, things that hold us back from our goals are called "limiting factors." These hurdles, bumps, or mountains in our way can be very frustrating—mostly because sometimes we just feel their impact and don't even know what they are. **Systems thinking teaches that our greatest power is not in working harder, but rather lies in our ability to identify and remove the limiting factors that hold us back.**

When we have a limited scope of reality, it is impossible for us to find where we have power or where other things have power over us. However, when we learn to think in this new way, we take on a new perspective that allows us to identify two things: (1) the leverage we possess for change and (2) the "noise" or limiting factors that hinder our movement from going forward. We tend to view the world in fragmented ways, but there is immense power in knowing and seeing reality in this holistic manner.

HERE COMES THE NOISE (LIMITING FACTORS)

It has been said that no plan survives the battlefield. Despite our best intentions and lofty visions, things don't always work out as planned.

The starlings in the Murmuration also have this problem. When starlings encounter forces that hinder their ability to fly acrobatically in unison, scientists call these factors "noise." Interestingly, research scientist Cavagna points out that in the Murmuration, "The key point is not the [behavioral] rule, but the noise. Given a reasonable behavioral rule . . . correlation strongly depends on the level of noise in implementing such a rule."[10] In other words, this is an echo of the systems thinking principle that our ability to reach our goal is not dependent as much on working harder (following behavioral rules), but the key point is in removing the things that hold us back (level of noise).

The reality is that our unified strategies will inevitably hit noise, barriers, and roadblocks of many kinds. And that's okay.

People are not perfect and sometimes make mistakes. Other times, external factors come into play that complicate what we are working toward. These external factors could be as simple as a technology failure that results in communication loss or complicated like a shift in government policy that changes strategies. These are the moments we need to rest in God's grace and allow Him to fill in the gaps. Whatever the "noise" is, our job is not to despair, but rather anticipate the noise, prepare as best we can, and trust our Father.

Our limiting factors to unity and the work of the Church work like a counterforce to the momentum we want and they can be extremely debilitating. The biggest limiting factor to unity is ultimately sin, but to just say sin is the root cause, though accurate, does not always help us move forward. There are many limiting factors to unity, but for space we focus here on what we believe to be two systemic limiting factors to disunity: mental structures and church structures.

Along with each limiting factor we identify, we also provide some ideas for how the Church can uproot each limiting factor. Christ calls us to ruthlessly cut off that which hinders us (Matthew 5:30), and that includes removing our limiting factors!

There are many things that hinder the Church from moving into the *completion* quadrant of our relationships and strategy matrix. We have outlined just two key factors below, but as you practice the discipline of seeing things in wholes, you will be able to identify more. As you do, please share your perspective—we need your contributions to the conversation.

LIMITING FACTORS TO A UNITY MOVEMENT: MENTAL STRUCTURES AND CHURCH STRUCTURES

Mental Structures

One of the main things that hinders unity in the Church today is the mental structures we hold. Mental structures are assumptions or generalizations that are deeply engrained in our thinking. These thoughts influence how we view our surroundings and consequently, how we move, live, and engage with others.

Within our mental structures, we have identified three common currents of thinking: pride, comfort, and fear. We also offer a few suggestions on how to remove these negative mental structures that hold the Church back from taking flight.

Our mental structures are limiting factors because they control our actions, *all beneath the surface*. This gets to the internal health of each individual. Unity will be limited severely when the personal mental models of believers are unhealthy.

Why did we react that way to that other pastor or ministry leader? Why are we harboring a grudge against a brother or sister in Christ? Why don't we trust *that* sort of Christian? We are not always sure how to answer these questions, but it always has something to do with our mental structures and how we think.

Jay Forrester, systems expert, points out that changing the decision-making procedures in people is much harder than anyone imagines.[11] Forrester and his team learned that merely a consultant coming into an organization and offering the proper systemic solutions would not solve any problems. This was true because individuals in organizations would revert back to their old way of thinking under the pressure of daily operations. So for us, sharing a compelling biblical vision with enthusiasm and optimism is just not enough; we need to also remove the wrong patterns and mental structures that limit us from unity.

It is paramount to point out that Forrester believes we should expose children as young as ten years old to systems dynamics and establish a strong sense of the cause and effect process in them before contrary patterns of thought are irrevocably established. This supports our belief that we must begin infusing our curriculums for children and youth with a biblical vision for unity. The content we offer children and youth is largely devoid of this message. When we elevate the importance of unity in their Christian worldview, it will create future leaders who can more easily help the Church murmurate for the expansion of the Kingdom!

Since logical arguments are not enough, we need God to sweep in and cause a *metanoia* in us. This Greek word appears in the New Testament twenty-two times and it refers to having a change in mind, typically associated with repentance (Matthew 3:8, Luke 5:32, Acts 5:31). This move of the heart and mind happens when we see how we were wrong and then turn from our old ways toward a better way: God's design. This change of mind and heart starts with *me* and *you*!

This will mean holding up the mirror to ourselves and rooting out a lack of forgiveness, grudges, resentment, and jealousy and asking ourselves if we might be the source to the "noise" currently limiting the Murmuration of the body of Christ.

Pride, comfort, and fear are some of the major mental structures that cause us devastating daily blows and limit the unity of God.

Pride

Pride (I am better than...) is one of the loudest "noises" that limit unity. Pride is a way of thinking, or a mental structure, that produces so many evils. It fuels the "gold-standard effect" we mentioned earlier (thinking that our group is better than theirs). Pride is also the source of passion without compassion. We sometimes develop a great level of passion for a specific mission, but if pride is in the driver's seat, we lose the ability to have compassion for others who do not think like us and have a hard time seeing things from the other's perspective.

Passion without compassion also appears in theological conversations or discussions. In pride, we begin to believe that we have everything figured out and we immediately discredit and devalue others with diverse perspectives.

In our pride, more often we would rather be right than unified. This also drives a competitive spirit where we either think we are better than others or we actively work to be better than them. Along these lines, Thomas Merton steers us in the right direction: "When we are truly ourselves, we lose most of the futile self-consciousness that keeps us constantly comparing ourselves with others in order to see how big we are."[12] We can truly be ourselves only in Christ, and He then gives us the ability to stop the comparison game.

So how do we work to remove this limiting factor? The greatest power to remove pride lies in finding our identity in

Christ. Yes, we may know Christ as the redeemer and sacrificial lamb for our sins, but do we also know Him as the master carpenter, come to remodel our entire world and inner person too? Christ's work on the cross means redeeming and remaking our identities as well. Once, we were lost in sin and idolatry—the essence of pride. Christ demolished this old mind-set and now replaces it with humility. We do not need to boost ourselves for any reason, because we realize we are not the main characters in the story. When our identity is found in Christ, we have nothing to prove, and our grounded identity will send pride to its grave. **We no longer need to be rivals.** It is not about how big or impressive *my* church or ministry can be, how many followers or likes I get, or how flashy our programs are. Like standing next to the sun with a candle, the closer we get to Christ, the more trivial our pride will seem.

Comfort

A colleague of mine once had a sign in her office that became a powerful tagline used commonly among the staff at The Gathering Place. It read: "There is no comfort in a growth zone and no growth in a comfort zone." Our staff used it as a motivation to do the hard things and pursue growth even if we knew it would make us uncomfortable.

It's nature: we will always choose comfort and the path of least resistance. Even though the easy choice might hurt us in the long run, we still prefer to choose comfort. I remember my parents asking me in middle school if I wanted to transfer to a better school, one that would give me a better education and more opportunities for college. I responded with a cool,

"Nah, I'm okay at my current school." We tend to make decisions based on how circumstance will make us *feel* rather than on what is right, or best for our growth. Since we at least know our current playground, we fear trying the better playground, no matter how big and incredible the new one promises to be.

We try to rationalize our choices, but at the root is just a laziness to get out of our comfort zone. In systems thinking, there is a rule that governs these sorts of decisions. Peter Senge states that rule in this way: "The easy way out usually leads back in."[13] The idea is that when we do not take the time to make difficult and uncomfortable decisions today, we eventually circle back and find ourselves with the same problems we had before.

The easy choice is to stay comfortably in our small homogeneous kingdoms. Church, do you want to do something powerful? Pursue unity. It will require getting uncomfortable, but the reward is worth the pursuit!

We talk so much about church growth in the Christian sphere, but the ironic part is that our desire to stay comfortable is killing growth, both personal and corporate church growth. The old adage "no pain no gain" applies. Without a willingness to be in awkward social situations or have difficult theology conversations, we will not grow. There is no growth in a comfort zone!

That is why the solution to break down the *comfort*-limiting factor is to develop a deep commitment for growth and learning. When God fills us with a genuine desire for personal growth, this will drive us beyond our addiction to comfort on our journey for greater knowledge and truth. A genuine desire for growth assumes there is no finish line to learning and that we do not know all there is to know. This passion for growth, paired with humility, will shatter the limiting walls of pride and comfort!

Fear

This type of fear is not the "scared of the dark" sort of fear, but rather the crippling power of worry, stress, doubt, or anxiety. Fear makes us wonder if we are good enough. It causes us to dread failure or rejection if anyone gets close enough to look behind the curtain. This fear holds us back from connecting with others because we are afraid of what our association might mean or fearful that others might let us down. This mental model paints us in a corner where we hold too tightly to what we have, afraid to lose our slice of the pie with anxiety of what tomorrow might bring.

The ultimate solution to fear of course is basking in God's love. It is perfect *love* that casts out all fear, not courage (1 John 4:18). God perfectly and relentlessly loves you. That fact commands all fear to vanish because we begin to trust in His Fatherly instincts. What do we have to lose!?

Baby steps in new relationships also change the mental structure of fear. We tend to fear whatever we do not know; through relationships, however, we know and become known. Eventually, we see that our dividing walls are not as tall as we thought they were.

We can uproot the limiting factors of pride, comfort, and fear by finding our identity in Christ, operating in God's love, and learning to see the world in circles rather than straight lines. Linear thinking produces reactive behavior to circumstances, but seeing circular patterns of impact will help us see the bigger picture to understand all the influencers.

Church Structures

Church structures also have massive influence on our decisions and behavior. The structures in the Church we are referring to are both the literal brick and mortar church structures and the "operating policies" that translate into perceptions, goals, rules, and norms. Our behavior is based on the structures built around us because although we may not be aware of it, structure is what produces behavior.[14]

We've all heard how unkempt environments, such as subways with graffiti, litter, and broken glass, tend to promote a higher crime rate. On the other hand, well-kept environments promote rules of law and civility. So if structure and context produce behavior, we have greater leverage in stopping crime by cleaning up the environment rather than arresting the individuals committing the crime.

The Church structure conversation is so important because it addresses again the deeper reasons for our disunity. It also means that small changes to our structure or environment can produce big behavioral changes. Unfortunately, we use the word "church" quite broadly to refer to our buildings, denominations, the church as a system, or the combined fellowship of Christ followers. All of these definitions have structures within them. As we consider the structure we operate in, we might find that we have built social and physical structures that inadvertently contribute toward divisive behavior rather than protecting the unity of the Spirit.

2 + 2 = 5

Sometimes, we get a result we don't want because of structure. Reinhold Niebuhr's research in *Moral Man and Immoral Society* found that despite individual unselfishness, group think transmutates individual unselfishness into selfishness![15] There is something that happens in group dynamics that can produce undesirable outcomes if we don't set up our church structures in the right way. Let's look at how our physical structures and operational structures act as limiting factors to unity.

Physical Structures

It was Winston Churchill who said, "At first we shape our buildings and afterwards they shape us."[16] If you walk into a massive dimly lit cathedral like the *Sagrada Familia* in Spain, you probably act very differently than when you walk into a church with bright lights, music, and videos playing.

As if by reflex, the spatial structures we inhabit change our actions. Our church buildings have a great deal of power over us. We take pride in their beauty and at times rightfully so—many of them are wonderful expressions of worship to God.

Our love of our church campus can be dangerous too. We run capital campaigns, cast the vision for years, and raise the funds. Then comes the period of actual construction, and anticipation builds for the whole church community. After the dedication and using the facilities, then typically comes the long season of paying off the debt, sometimes even running two to three more capital campaigns to complete the project.

Whew! Building our physical church structures can easily be a ten- to twenty-year project with major dollars invested.

It is easy to see how such a large investment can become a major part of a church's identity, sometimes even appearing on the church logo. But what does that communicate about who we are and what we value? Sometimes our buildings force us to bring people to "us," and the geographical locations of our structures can limit our ability to build unity based on where they are located—in the countryside, the suburbs, or in urban locales. Our structures can be powerful tools for the Gospel, but we must identify their limitations. They can also be anchors that hold us back from freely moving and staying adaptive and agile like the Murmuration.

Have we ever considered that our church buildings themselves could potentially be a divisive element in our relationship with other believers? Asking ourselves how literal brick and mortar church structures affect our behavior is a difficult but wonderful question to explore.

Operational Structures

Operational structures are the ways that we run our ministries and churches. On the macro level, denominations are our operational structures. On the micro level, it is how we make decisions as a local congregation (Is leadership top down from the pastor? Is it through a team of elders? Is it one powerful church member? Is it anyone who happens to be holding the mic?). The operational structures can be the types of programs we design or also the operating policies in place within our organizations or denominational rules; they communicate what we value and how to be "normal" in a certain atmosphere.

These structures determine the behavioral norms that tells us how to speak, dress, and act in certain situations. If you are not aware of certain operational structures in a cultural context different from yours, this can make you feel extremely out of place. You may have felt this while on a mission trip or visiting a different country.

Another operational structure is the type of music we play or listen to. Music is an incredibly powerful force and can make people feel welcome and at home or totally out of place. I had to learn this lesson through receiving feedback after one of our staff meetings. To craft programs that engage students from diverse backgrounds, we intentionally maintain a diverse staff to get different perspectives on structures and the culture of our audience. Our small team at the time was about 50 percent white and the rest a mix of Indian, African American, and Hispanic. During our staff meetings, I periodically play worship music and we spend a few minutes praying and worshipping together. After one of those staff meetings, John, my friend and fellow staff member, shared how he felt it more difficult to connect during our worship times together because I don't play any music he is used to worshipping with.

Wow. It hit me that this was an operational structure that was subtle, but limiting our team. We must strive to not only be diverse in our makeup, but also in our expression. You can be sure I downloaded some different music onto my tablet and next time we worshipped together, he noticed the change and made it a point to express his thanks to the whole team. The way we actually operate internally in our ministries makes a big difference!

Some of these elements may not be negative on their own. We could even say that some structures are benign and only cultural, not really contributing to the disunity of the body. However, we must remember that in systems thinking, behavior is an outgrowth of structure. We may find ourselves in conflict with other believers over what we believe to be valid conflict, but in reality, it's just a clash of our cultures or operating structures. Unchecked, these structures produce *extremes* within our churches, limiting our unity.

A SOLUTION FOR NEGATIVE PHYSICAL AND OPERATIONAL STRUCTURES

Feedback. One of the ways we can unearth how our structures limit unity is by finding people who can give feedback—the right kind of *compassionate* feedback. These sources of feedback must be diverse, coming from a different perspective or paradigm than our own. Getting good feedback means it must have three elements: honest, have a solid handle and perspective on your life/work/context, and be delivered with incredible compassion.

Finding a source for this kind of feedback is one of the most precious assets you can cultivate, but it must be matched with the humility necessary to receive the feedback. Research shows that psychologically, we are not willing to receive this sort of feedback from those in our "out-group" or those who are different from us.[17] To find and receive this feedback from believers who are diverse, it will require changing our ideas about others and including them in our definition of "us." Feedback is a powerful strategy for pulling back our blinders to see beyond our limited perspective.

Consider the old Eastern tale about three blind men who encounter an elephant. When they walk up to the elephant, each one describes his perspective of the broad animal. The first, grabbing the ear, is convinced the animal is broad and flat, much like a rug. The second man takes hold of the trunk and says to the first man, "No way, this animal is long and round and strong." Finally, the third man chimes in, holding a leg, saying, "You are both wrong; this beast is strong and massive like a tree." Are we not like these blind men if we do not cultivate the feedback and perspective our brothers and sisters in Christ can offer?

The Church has a problem with seeing "whole elephants." Stuck in our mental structures and church structures, we become deaf to the valuable feedback and perspective of other believers. Wouldn't it be a shame if we missed the majesty of the whole Murmuration because we were so fixated on one bird? Wouldn't it be a shame if we missed the power of the Body of Christ because we didn't welcome the perspectives of other believers?

Without knowing your particular context, we are not necessarily prescribing a specific structure change. Remember that today's solutions can cause tomorrow's problems, so make any structural change you might consider carefully, slowly, and with a systematic perspective. None of us has all of the answers to what structural changes must occur—we all have limited perspectives and that is why this must be a shared project. No one individual can diagnose the underlying structures of the system of the church and know where to apply this leverage.

We all need memorable and practical reference points on a journey. As you live the Murmuration principles, there will be moments you might get discouraged or disoriented. That is when you need to remember the rules to live by to keep you grounded.

These rules are all about shifting the way we think and the way we see ourselves and the world—from seeing ourselves as reactors to active shapers of our future. Real change comes when people realize that the first step is changing the way we think. This happens fundamentally when we engage in prayer and dependence on the Holy Spirit and allow God to renew our minds. When our work hits reality and life's limiting factors slow us down, we cannot forget to keep it simple because small changes can have big results. Finally, when the climb seems too steep or the hurdles too high, remember that our greatest leverage is in *removing* our limiting factors rather than working harder to climb the mountain or jump the hurdles.

An awe-inspiring element of the Murmuration phenomenon is that the birds are *most effective* at their formation when they follow their behavioral rules **even when there is a lot of** "**noise.**" They don't work harder at it, they just remain consistent and true even when it gets tough. Even when there is a full force headwind, they follow the vision. Even when your neighbor is sick and not flying at full capacity, follow the vision. Even when your predator is coming right at *you*, follow the vision. For us, living these rules will allow us to be a body that creates the future God wants.

Chapter 14

Let's GO!

You ask, what is our aim? I can answer in one word: Victory. Victory at all costs—Victory in spite of all terror—Victory, however long and hard the road may be, for without victory there is no survival.

—Winston Churchill, May 13, 1940;
The House of Commons

The revolution awaits us.

The sky is our empty canvas, waiting for the brush strokes of the Holy Spirit as He conducts a broad sweeping Murmuration of the global Church. The movement only needs a critical mass of believers who catch God's passion for unity, pushing us beyond our holding patterns and into our highest potential.

The time is now. Division in the Church has held back the mission of God for too long. He designed us for so much more, but disunity among Christians continues to dramatically limit our fullest potential.

232 PRACTICAL STEPS TO HELP SPARK A MOVEMENT

Our calling is too critical for us to continue settling for smaller playgrounds. Not only do we miss the personal blessings of a united Christian community, but the world continues to languish, waiting for the people of God. If we want to be the powerful agent for change we were designed to be, then we must fight for unity.

Nothing will change until we first identify the current state of division and simultaneously catch Jesus' vision for the Church to be *as one as the Trinity*. The ability to perceive both our status quo and Christ's vision will propel us forward through creative tension. But this momentum-generating perspective will need a practical road map and a little extra horse-power; this is where the Murmuration principles come in.

With a clear picture of our reality and the biblical vision for unity, we are then ready to live the Murmuration principles: Seven Influential Neighbors, Collective Strategy—Focus on the Common Enemy, Critical Mass, Recognition of Mutual Need, There Is No Alpha, Divide You Die, and Contribution.

Learning and living these lessons will require on-the-job training of the systems thinking discipline to reshape the way we think and perceive the interconnectedness of our world. With this new discipline and a daily dose of faith and optimism, we will stand as ready leaders to spark a MOvement!

We cannot just keep this new perspective to ourselves either. The unity Christ desires begins in our hearts and mind, but must also manifest in the physical world. We need to be daring evangelists to our own brothers and sisters in Christ with this vision and build the critical mass needed to start a movement.

We must never forget that ultimately unity is not just for unity's sake, but also for what it produces. In other words, unity reflects who God is and also turns into something special; collective citywide strategies based on relationships, diverse perspectives, and a systems approach to solving our greatest problems. This sort of movement, led by bold, focused, and humble leaders, is going to be like nothing we have ever seen before. Once we get a taste of what *completion* feels like, we will come back thirsty for more. We will recognize just how much we truly need one another and how anemic we were before we invited others into our sphere.

The engines that pull us out of *competition* and toward *completion* are the two key building blocks for unity: relationships and common strategy growing at the same time. This is when our Seven Influential Neighbors play a significant role in the process, helping us navigate toward unity despite very real differences we might have. God has given us a road map for overcoming any obstacle with this guiding framework. Like the dabbawalas, we can have no excuses!

Birds first taught us how to fly and now they will teach us how to unify—and help the Church soar to new heights!

We hope the thoughts and ideas we have shared have been challenging and encouraging. We hope you have heard our hearts and felt the great love we have for the Church and our desire for us to be better together. But this book cannot be just about nice ideas—God wants a stirring in the hearts of His people that turns tangible! In this final chapter, we offer three simple next steps you can take to get momentum going: pick up the phone; own the vision; be stubborn about unity.

PICK UP THE PHONE

Yep. The path to unity can really be as simple as a phone call. But don't just skip to the next heading so fast.

Living into our design requires initiative. A willingness to think and work outside the normal paths we are accustomed to following. Consider how many other ministries or churches are in your vicinity. Are there other Christians in your neighborhood or at work? Do you have relationships with individuals that are from diverse backgrounds or diverse ways of thinking? Maybe you *are* the pastor—do you have regular relationship and strategy-building conversations with the leadership of the church to your right? To your left? Across the street? Across town?

If you answered yes to some of those questions, that's awesome—keep pressing into relationships. If you struggled to find a yes, or maybe the questions themselves were totally new ideas, then there is great opportunity for growth. The issues and challenges are daunting, but the opportunities are so much bigger!

One phone call can change a *no* to a *yes*. Someone has to *initiate* the relationship. Period. Unity and relationships are not going to happen on their own without an active fight against the enemy's strategy to divide the Church.

Maybe you could even pick up the phone right now—if you're on leadership at a church, reach out to a neighboring ministry. If you are a church member, call your church leadership and begin a conversation about becoming a murmurating church—you can even offer to work through this book together with the key stakeholders you identify.

Nervous about the phone call? Unity matters to Jesus and our relationships are the secret sauce for unity.[1] Just go for it and initiate the relationship!

OWN THE VISION

You play a vital role in unleashing Christ's vision for unity. Remember that *any* bird can initiate change or create movement in the Murmuration! We do not need to wait for one alpha to lead the way—just like the starlings, every single one of us has the ability to initiate a movement and create change! You have a limitless amount of potential inside of you to help spark unity in the Church. As a follower of Jesus, the limitless God of creation dwells in you and invites you to contribute to His Kingdom.

When working on a house or carpentry project, sometimes my children want to help. The truth is, when they are involved, it either slows me down or causes some sort of major spill or setback. **But I allow them to help because in the end, we did it together.** This is how I think God must feel about us. Even though we don't always get it right or perfect, He does it *with* us. Our loving Father has invited us to be co-laborers with Him in the most exciting project of all time—so let's take ownership of it.

Owning the vision means getting to work and also helping others have a MOment too. Don't wait for someone else to take responsibility. Let's each own the vision, share the message, and not wait around for anyone else to lead.

MIKE'S STORY

When we own the vision for unity ourselves, we will be able to help our communities *envision, attempt, and accomplish* more. A common theme that you may sense throughout many of the stories in this book is that when Christians come together, we have the possibility to do more together than if we work on our own. We all long to be part of something bigger than ourselves and through faith in Christ, we are.

Envision

When we come together, it's amazing what fresh eyes can bring to the table. We are often too close to our own work and we need a new look from a fresh heart to come alongside us. I've been in many meetings where I've seen new ideas presented that I had never thought of. Fresh perspective sees things that can make a vision so much bigger and better.

Attempt

When we bring the strengths of individuals and organizations together, we can attempt so much more together because of our multiplied resources. That's what happened with the Overtime story we shared earlier. Who would have thought that Sea World would allow us to use their venue for an outreach event where thousands of students would be exposed to the Gospel? Who would have thought that six thousand students would show up after football games on a Friday night? This was possible only because our relationships allowed us to attempt more!

Accomplish

When we dream together and bring our best to the table, it's amazing what God can accomplish through us.

The dream began in another one of those meetings where leaders from around the country had come together for our annual ministry council meeting with the National Network of Youth Ministries.

We were asking the question: "Where is God working and how could we join Him?"

I can remember breaking off in small groups around the home where we were meeting. We began to discuss what it would look like to bring together more youth ministry leaders for training and accomplishing the vision of reaching more teenagers with the Gospel. We envisioned a time when these youth ministries could participate in training and then in the evening they could join with others to celebrate what God was doing in the lives of thousands of students throughout the nation.

After a number of follow-up conversations and following God's leading, we found ourselves gathered in Atlanta at the Georgia Dome in 1996, on the front end of the Promise Keepers Clergy conference. From a few living room conversations, here we were getting ready to welcome leaders from all over the nation into a stadium to come together for the Gospel.

Over eight thousand youth leaders from all over the country representing many denominations, para-church ministries, and local churches found themselves side by side worshipping and celebrating what God was presently doing, praying together for future generations of teenagers to come. It was an amazing time in the history of youth ministry.

BE STUBBORN ABOUT UNITY

We have no excuse for being passive about Christ's vision. Unity is not optional.

Our world is deeply divided and is crying out for answers. If the summing up of all things in heaven and earth is God's design through the cross (Ephesians 1), then we cannot for a moment go soft on this biblical imperative. The desire of our Lord should compel us to stay the course and fight for unity and collective movement.

Let's shift the conversation from what people *won't do* to what they *will do*. With pure motives, it is time to get uncomfortable for the sake of the Gospel and move beyond the convenience of our four walls. Such a culture change will demand a certain level of stubbornness and repetition for a new language to take root in the Church. Bring it up in staff meetings. If you lead a small group or ever have to lead a devotional, launch from one of the many passages in the Bible about unity. If you have authority over job descriptions, write in a responsibility to build collaborative relationships. Share this book with your book club. Lead your family and children in discussions about unity. If you are a teacher, find ways to include this message in your syllabus. The opportunities are endless. The fact is, our mainstream Christian culture and schools are so devoid of this message that any leadership in this direction will be a fresh wind for the Church.

Being stubborn also means not giving up when things get tough. In the face of limiting factors, skeptics, and your weaker brothers and sisters, stay the course! Our world is waiting for bold leaders, willing to be ridiculed, even scorned because of their intense belief in Christ's vision for unity. Unity deeply matters to God, so why would we go in any direction other than God's design?

LET'S GO!

The orphan child and widow. The hungry family. The spiritually lost. The sick, outcast, and oppressed. They are all waiting for the Church to live in God's greater design. For us to have widespread impact on the massive problems that afflict our world, we need the Christian community to explode into a Murmuration!

How much longer must the world wait for the unleashing of the power of the Church? We do not have a single minute to waste. Our fellowship is one brimming with possibility, gifts, talents, and resources that a hurting world desperately needs. We are the light, but shining as individual rays in different directions, we have not yet caught the world's attention.

Let's unite into one bright beacon shining bright in the darkness. Like learning a new language or like an infant learning to walk, it will be difficult at first, but then it will become second nature through the power of the Spirit.

Today is a fresh day and anything is possible.

It is time to activate and share the vision. It doesn't really mean much to believe God calls us to unity until our convictions actually change the way we live. The power of the Gospel to unite is immeasurable, and we cannot stifle that power by allowing the brokenness and pain of the past to corrupt the future! What might seem impossible for us, God can do in one instant, and what seems lost to us, God can rescue in a moment. May we allow God's restorative power to heal old wounds and uproot bitterness and distrust.

Now is that time.

If we lay hold of Christ's design for unity and begin to actually live it out, believers will open the floodgates for the mission of the Church like never before. The world will watch with jaw-dropping wonder at our Murmuration, and in the end see Christ.

Acknowledgments

Lucas Ramirez

First and foremost, I want to thank God for the gift of Jesus and the gift of belonging to His Church.

My gratitude to my wife, Thea. You are a blessing to me beyond measure, and it was your encouragement, edits, and our many conversations that served as a crucible to refine these ideas.

I want to thank my partner in this project, Mike DeVito. Our countless video conference calls, whiteboard sessions, and prayer times together were a blast. This book is so much better because of your contribution, and I'm a better man because of your investment in me.

A very special thanks to Tyler Reagin and the Catalyst Team. Your invitation to share this vision on your platform propelled this entire book forward in immeasurable ways.

My gratitude to Lisa Jackson and the Alive Literary Team. Your expertise helped refine our flow and content. I'm lucky to have such a genuine, committed, and gifted agent.

A huge debt of gratitude is owed to our editor Keren Baltzer and the entire FaithWords publishing team. I can't express how thankful I am to you for believing in this message. Thank you for making the text really sing and investing your talent to propel this vision forward!

A big thank-you to my team and leadership board at The Gathering Place—it is an honor to labor for the Lord shoulder to shoulder with you. Thank you to all of our endorsers and to so many other connectors, mentors, teachers, and cheerleaders such as Mark and Cindi Sholander, Duffy Robbins, N. T. Wright, the Pflug family (especially our intern Jack!), my friends at iMint media, Esther Fleece, Beckie Manly, Chris Cox, Shelene Bryan, Jay Hanson, Bill Walker, and many more. You each propelled this project at critical phases or sharpened our thinking.

Lastly, I want to thank my parents, Eduardo and Elvira. Your love, mentorship, and intentionality have made me the leader I am today. Thank you for such a rich legacy.

Mike DeVito

My thanks to Lucas Ramirez for believing together that churches can murmurate the heart of God to our broken world and for inviting me on this unbelievably wild ride. My gratitude to Brian Cress from International Justice Mission who first introduced me to Lucas. I am deeply grateful for the National Network of Youth Ministries team who continues to champion the cause of unity across the nation and for the faithful City Coordinators of the Southwest Region who keep the vision for unity alive day by day in the trenches. Finally, my heartfelt thanks to Pastor Denny Davis who gave me my first youth ministry position, who modeled and encouraged me to be part of something bigger than just one church or denomination.

Notes

Chapter 1. The Murmuration

1 Edmund Selous, *Bird Life Glimpses* (London: G. Allen, 1905), 141.

2 According to the Royal Society for Protection of Birds, Murmurations can have 100k+ starlings: https://www.rspb.org.uk/birds-and-wildlife/wildlife-guides/bird-a-z/starling/starling-Murmurations

3 Mehrdad Baghai, James Quibley, et al., *As One: Individual Action, Collective Power* (New York: Portfolio / Penguin, 2011). Print.

4 Peter M. Senge, *The Fifth Discipline: The Art and Practice of the Learning Organization* (New York: Doubleday Currency, 1990), 69. *ATLA Religion Database with ATLASerials.*

5 Ravi Zacharias reference: http://rzim.org/just-thinking/the-inextinguishable-light/.

6 John H. Armstrong, *Your Church Is Too Small: Why Unity in Christ's Mission Is Vital to the Future of the Church* (Grand Rapids, MI: Zondervan, 2010), 52.

7 Senge, *The Fifth Discipline*, 132.

8 Ibid., 140.

9 David B. Barrett, *World Christian Encyclopedia: A Comparative Study of Churches and Religion in the Modern World, AD 1900–2000*, 2nd edition (Oxford; New York: Oxford University Press, 2001). http://www.gordonconwell.edu/resources/Center-for-the-Study-of-Global-Christianity.cfm.

10 Geoffrey Wainwright, et al., *Ecumenical Theology in Worship, Doc-trine, and Life: Essays Presented to Geoffrey Wainwright on His Sixtieth Birthday* (New York: Oxford University Press, 1999). From Norman Young essay: *Sacrament, Sign and Unity*, quoting Cardinal Hume.

Chapter 2. Designed for Bigger, Better Playgrounds

1 Sarah Hinlicky Wilson, "Lament for a Divided Church," *Christian-ity Today* 58, No. 2 (March 2014): 36. http://www.christianitytoday.com/ct/2014/march/lament-for-divided-church.html?paging=off.

2 C. Lincoln and L. Mamiya, *The Black Church in the African American Experience* [e-book] (Durham, NC: Duke University Press, 1990), xii. ATLA Religion Database with ATLASerials, Ipswich, MA.

3 Christian Smith and Michael O. Emerson, *Divided by Faith: Evan-gelical Religion and the Problem of Race in America* (Oxford: Oxford University Press, 2000), 16–18. ATLA Religion Database with ATLASerials. Web. August 20, 2015.

4 N. T. Wright, "In Full Accord," *Christian Century* 128.5 (2011): 25–29. Humanities International Index. Web. June 20, 2015.

5 Christena Cleveland, *Disunity in Christ: Uncovering the Hidden Forces That Keep Us Apart* (Downers Grove, IL: IVP Books, 2013), 27, 28.

6 David B. Barrett, *World Christian Encyclopedia: A Comparative Study of Churches and Religion in the Modern World AD 1900–2000*, 2nd edition (New York: Oxford University Press, 2001). http://www.gordoncon well.edu/resources/Center-for-the-Study-of-Global-Christianity.cfm.

7 Cleveland, *Disunity*, 29.

8 Story on IJM historic unity: https://www.ijm.org/news/historic -interfaith-movement-against-human-trafficking-launched -philippines.

9 Cleveland, *Disunity*, 27, 28.

10 Albert H. Hastorf and Hadley Cantril, "They Saw a Game: A Case Study," *The Journal of Abnormal and Social Psychology* 49.1 (1954): 129–134. PsycARTICLES. Web. August 19, 2015.

11 Mark R. Leary, "Self and Motivation: Emerging Psychological Perspectives," in *When Selves Collide: The Nature of the Self and the Dynamics of Interpersonal Relationships*, 119–145 (Washington, DC: American Psychological Association, 2002). PsycINFO.

12 Ibid.

13 Ibid.

14 Cleveland, *Disunity*, 70.

15 Smith and Emerson, *Divided by Faith*, 158.

16 Ibid., 151.

17 Adam Smith, *Wealth of Nations* (Hoboken, NJ: Generic NL Freebook Publisher, n.d.), 162. eBook Collection (EBSCOhost). Web. August 20, 2015.

18 These thoughts came from a lunch conversation with my friend and economics professor Dr. Skip Mounts

19 Perspective on Jewish culture: https://www.thattheworldmay know.com/rabbi-and-talmidim.

20 N. T. Wright, "In Full Accord," *Christian Century* 128.5 (2011): 25–29. Humanities International Index.

21 A personal interview with N. T. Wright, Zest Cafe, St. Andrews, Scotland, December 8, 2017.

22 John H. Armstrong, *Your Church Is Too Small: Why Unity in Christ's Mission Is Vital to the Future of the Church* (Grand Rapids, MI: Zondervan, 2010), 19. ATLA Religion Database with ATLASerials.

23 Ibid., 36.

24 Leary, "Self and Motivation," 119–145.

25 Cleveland, *Disunity*, 63.

Chapter 3. God's Vision for Unity

1 N. T. Wright, *John for Everyone*. Part 2: chapters 11–21 (London: Society for Promoting Christian Knowledge, 2004), 93.

2 N. T. Wright, *Simply Christian: Why Christianity Makes Sense* (New York: HarperCollins, 2006).

3 Donald Guthrie, *Galatians* (London: Thomas Nelson & Sons, 1969), 115.

4 Rene Padilla, "The Nature and Mission of the Church: The Case for Unity," *Evangelical Review of Theology* 7, No. 2 (October 1983– March 1984): 5–6.

5 N. T. Wright, "In Full Accord," *Christian Century* 128.5 (2011): 25– 29. Humanities International Index. Web. June 20, 2015.

6 Padilla, "The Nature," 20.

7 https://www.biblicaltraining.org/library/trinity-wayne-grudem.

8 Ian C. Bradley, *The Celtic Way* (London: Darton Longman & Todd, 2003).

9 Sarah Hinlicky Wilson, "Lament for a Divided Church," *Christianity Today* 58, No. 2 (March 2014): 36. http://www.christianitytoday .com/ct/2014/march/lament-for-divided-church.html?paging=off.

10 Patrick Frank and Duane Preble, *Prebles Artforms: An Introduction to the Visual Arts* (Upper Saddle River, NJ: Pearson, 2014), 72–75.

11 David A. Lauer and Stephen Pentak, *Design Basics,* 9th edition (Boston: Cengage, 2015), 30.

12 Wayne Grudem's Systematic Theology podcast—*The Purity and Unity of the Church*, December 31, 2000—Apologetics315.com.

13 Ben Witherington III, *John's Wisdom: A Commentary on the Fourth Gospel* (Louisville, KY: Westminster, 1995), 274.

Chapter 4. Principle 1: Seven Influential Neighbors

1 Keynote at Catalyst Conference, March 2017.

2 Wayne Potts, "The Chorus-Line Hypothesis of Manoeuvre Coordination in Avian Flocks," *Nature* 309, No. 5967 (May 24, 1984): 344–345.

3 M. Ballerini, V. Cabibbo, R. Candelier, E. Cisbani, I. Giardina, V. Lecomte, et al., "Interaction Ruling Animal Collective Behavior Depends on Topological Rather Than Metric Distance: Evidence from a Field Study," *Proceedings of the National Academy of Science,* 105 (2008b): 1232–1237.

4 Jennifer Ackerman, *The Genius of Birds* (New York: Corsair, 2017), 101.

5 N. T. Wright, "In Full Accord," *Christian Century* 128.5 (2011): 25–29. Humanities International Index. Web. June 20, 2015.

6 Christena Cleveland, *Disunity in Christ: Uncovering the Hidden Forces That Keep Us Apart* (Downers Grove, IL: IVP Books, 2013), 30, 31, 56.

7 Erica J. Boothby, Margaret S. Clark, and John A. Bargh, "Shared Experiences Are Amplified," *Psychological Science* 25.12 (2014): 2209–2216. Business Source Premier. Web. September 3, 2015.

8 Diversity Dividend: http://www.mckinsey.com/business-functions/organization/our-insights/why-diversity-matters.

9 Patrick M. Lencioni, *The Five Dysfunctions of a Team* (Hoboken, NJ: Wiley-Blackwell, 2010).

10 Competition vs. Completion matrix adapted from a Harvard Business Review article.

11 Andrea Cavagna, Alessio Cimarelli, Irene Giardina, Giorgio Parisi, Raffaele Santagati, Fabio Stefanini, et al., "Scale-Free Correlations in Starling Flocks," *PNAS Proceedings of the National Academy of Sciences of the United States of America* 107.26 (2010): 11865–11870. PsycINFO.

Chapter 5. Principle 2: Collective Strategy—Focus on the Common Enemy

1 Miroslav Volf, *Exclusion and Embrace: A Theological Exploration of Identity, Otherness, and Reconciliation* (Nashville, TN: Abingdon Press, 1996). ProQuest ebrary. Web. September 9, 2015.

2 A. E. Goodenough, N. Little, W. S. Carpenter, and A. G. Hart, "Birds of a Feather Flock Together: Insights into Starling Murmuration Behaviour Revealed Using Citizen Science," *PLoS ONE* 12(6): e0179277. https://doi.org/10.1371/journal.pone.0179277.

3 Jennifer Ackerman, *The Genius of Birds* (New York: Corsair, 2017), 113.

4 Goodenough, "Birds of a Feather."

5 Robert Slocum, *Engaging the Spirit: Essays on the Life and Theology of the Holy Spirit* (New York: Church Publishing, 2001), 68.

6 Phillip Butler, *Well Connected: Releasing Power and Restoring Hope Through Kingdom Partnerships* (Colorado Springs, CO: Authentic Publishing, 2006).

Chapter 6. Principle 3: Critical Mass

1 David Platt, *Radical Together, Unleashing the People of God for the Purpose of God* (Colorado Springs, CO: Multnomah, 2011).

2 https://en.wikipedia.org/wiki/Critical_point_(thermodynamics) critical point. (n.d.). Dictionary.com Unabridged. Retrieved August 19, 2017, from Dictionary.com website http://www.dictionary.com/browse/critical-point.

3 https://en.wikipedia.org/wiki/Phase_(matter).

4 Andrea Cavagna, Alessio Cimarelli, Irene Giardina, Giorgio Parisi, Raffaele Santagati, Fabio Stefanini, et al., "Scale-Free Correlations in Starling Flocks," *PNAS* 107 No. 26 (2010): 11865–11870; published ahead of print June 14, 2010. doi:10.1073/pnas.1005766107. Page 11866.

5 Ibid., 11869.

6 T. Niizato and Y.-P. Gunji, "Fluctuation-Driven Flocking Movement in Three Dimensions and Scale-Free Correlation," *PLoS ONE* 7, No. 5 (2012): e35615. doi:10.1371/ journal.pone.0035615.

7 A. E. Goodenough, N. Little, W. S. Carpenter, and A. G. Hart, "Birds of a Feather Flock Together: Insights into Starling Murmuration Behaviour Revealed Using Citizen Science, *PLoS ONE* 12, No. 6 (2017): e0179277. https://doi.org/10.1371/journal. Pone.0179277.

8 M. Ballerini, N. Cabibbo, R. Candelier, A. Cavagna, E. Cisbani, I. Giardina, et al., "Empirical Investigation of Starling Flocks: A Benchmark Study in Collective Animal Behaviour," *Animal Behavior* 76 (2008): 201–215.

9 Andrea Cavagna, Alessio Cimarelli, Irene Giardina, Giorgio Parisi, Raffaele Santagati, Fabio Stefanini, et al., "From Empirical Data to Inter-Individual Interactions: Unveiling the Rules of Collective

Animal Behavior," *Mathematical Models and Methods in Applied Sciences* 20 (2010): 1491–1510.

10 Malcolm Gladwell, *The Tipping Point: How Little Things Can Make a Big Difference* (Boston: Little, Brown, 2000), 12.

Chapter 7. Principle 4: Recognition of Mutual Need

1 Andrea Cavagna, Alessio Cimarelli, Irene Giardina, Giorgio Parisi, Raffaele Santagati, Fabio Stefanini, et al., "Scale-Free Correlations in Starling Flocks," *PNAS* 107, No. 26 (2010): 11865–11870; published ahead of print June 14, 2010, doi:10.1073/pnas.1005766107. Page 11869.

2 Ibid., 11866.

3 T. Niizato and Y.-P. Gunji, "Fluctuation-Driven Flocking Movement in Three Dimensions and Scale-Free Correlation," *PLoS ONE* 7, No. 5 (2012): e35615. doi:10.1371/journal.ponc.0035615. Page 2.

4 Cavagna et al., "Scale-Free Correlations," 11866.

5 Kerysso. https://www.blueletterbible.org/search/search.cfm?Criteria=preach&t=NIV#s=s_primary_0_.

6 N. T. Wright, *Simply Jesus: A New Vision of Who He Was and Why He Matters* (San Francisco: HarperOne, 2011), 193.

7 Tom Wright, *John for Everyone, Part 2: Chapters 11–21* (London: Society for Promoting Christian Knowledge, 2004), 140–143.

8 Dennis Sherwood, *Seeing the Forest for the Trees: A Manager's Guide to Applying Systems Thinking* (Yarmouth, ME: Nicholas Brealey Publishing, 2002). ProQuest ebrary. Web. August 25, 2015.

9 Peter M. Senge, *The Fifth Discipline: The Art and Practice of the Learning Organization* (New York: Doubleday, 1990), 5–10.

10 Ibid., 1.

11 Jay W. Forrester, "The Beginning of System Dynamics," *McKinsey Quarterly* 4 (1995): 4–16. Business Source Premier. Web. August 25, 2015.

12 John H. Armstrong, *Your Church Is Too Small: Why Unity in Christ's Mission Is Vital to the Future of the Church* (Grand Rapids, MI: Zondervan, 2010). ATLA Religion Database with ATLASerials. Page 13.

13 Senge, "The Fifth Discipline," 40.

14 Dietrich Bonhoeffer, *Life Together: The Classic Exploration of Christian Community* (New York: Harper & Row, 1954), 21.

Chapter 8. Principle 5: There Is No Alpha

1 Thomas Merton, *No Man Is An Island* (Wilmington, MA: Mariner Books, 2002).

2 Wayne Potts, "Nature," *Macmillan Journals* 309, No. 5967 (May 1984): 344–345.

3 Ibid.

4 Andrea Cavagna, Alessio Cimarelli, Irene Giardina, Giorgio Parisi, Raffaele Santagati, Fabio Stefanini, et al., "Scale-Free Correlations in Starling Flocks," *PNAS* 107, No. 26 (2010). www.pnas.org/cgi/doi/10.1073/pnas.1005766107.

5 Phillip Butler, *Well Connected: Releasing Power and Restoring Hope Through Kingdom Partnerships* (Colorado Springs, CO: Authentic Publishing, 2006), 201.

6 Jim Collins, *Good to Great: Why Some Companies Make the Leap... and Others Don't* (New York: Random House, 2001).

7 Mike Breen and Steve Cockram, *Building a Discipling Culture: How to Release a Missional Movement by Discipling People Like Jesus Did* (Kindle: 3DM, 2014), 52.

8 Collins, *Good to Great*, 30.

9 The six steps are loosely based on John Kotter's eight steps for leading change in any organization. John Kotter is a globally recognized management thinker and professor emeritus at Harvard University. Check out his book, *Leading Change*.

10 Andy Stanley, *Visioneering: Your Guide for Discovering and Maintaining Personal Vision* (Colorado Springs, CO: Multnomah, 2016), 260.

11 Thomas Merton, *New Seeds of Contemplation* (New York: New Directions, 2007), 142–149.

Chapter 9. Principle 6: Divide You Die

1 A. E. Goodenough, N. Little, W. S. Carpenter, and A. G. Hart, "Birds of a Feather Flock Together: Insights into Starling Murmuration Behaviour Revealed Using Citizen Science, *PLoS ONE* 12, No. 6 (2017): 3. https://doi.org/10.1371/journal; pone.0179277.

2 Rene Padilla, "The Nature and Mission of the Church: The Case for Unity," *Evangelical Review of Theology* 7, No. 2 (October 1983–March 1984): 5–6.

3 Sarah Hinlicky Wilson, "Lament for a Divided Church," *Christianity Today* 58, No. 2 (March 2014): 36. http://www.christianitytoday.com/ct/2014/march/lament-for-divided-church.html?paging=off.

4 Peter M. Senge, *The Fifth Discipline: The Art and Practice of the Learning Organization* (New York: Doubleday, 1990).

5 Vivian Loh, laikuen@sji.edu.sg, "The Power of Collaborative Dialogue," *Art Education* 68.5 (2015): 14–19. OmniFile Full Text Select (H. W. Wilson). Web. September 8, 2015.

6 Clinton Golding, "We Made Progress: Collective Epistemic Progress in Dialogue Without Consensus," *Journal of Philosophy of Education* 47.3 (2013): 423–440. Professional Development Collection. Web. September 8, 2015.

7 Richard Mouw, *Adventures in Evangelical Civility* (Grand Rapids, MI: Brazos Press, 2016), 4.

8 Brenda Salter McNeil, *Roadmap to Reconciliation: Moving Communities into Unity, Wholeness, and Justice* (Downers Grove, IL: Intervarsity Press, 2015), 71–72.

9 Miroslav Volf, *Exclusion and Embrace: A Theological Exploration of Identity, Otherness, and Reconciliation* (Nashville, TN: Abingdon Press, 1996), 129. ProQuest ebrary. Web. September 9, 2015.

10 See John Watson quote in John H. Armstrong, *Your Church Is Too Small: Why Unity in Christ's Mission Is Vital to the Future of the Church* (Grand Rapids, MI: Zondervan, 2010), 34.

11 Scott Sauls, *Jesus Outside the Lines: A Way Forward for Those Who Are Tired of Taking Sides* (Carol Stream, IL: Tyndale House Publishers, 2015), 4.

12 Volf, *Exclusion and Embrace*, 37–38.

13 N. T. Wright, *The Last Word: Scripture and the Authority of God—Getting Beyond the Bible Wars* (New York: HarperCollins, 2006), 24.

14 Ibid., 28.

15 Ibid., xi.

16 Ibid., 45.

17 Ibid., 31.

18 Notes from February 3, 2015, Podcast from N. T. Wright interview: *Justification and New Perspective on Paul.*

19 Sarah Hinlicky Wilson, "Lament for a Divided Church," *Christianity Today* 58, No. 2 (March 2014): 36. http://www.christianitytoday.com /ct/2014/march/lament-for-divided-church.html?paging=off.

20 Christena Cleveland, *Disunity in Christ: Uncovering the Hidden Forces That Keep Us Apart* (Westmont, IL: IVP Books, 2013), 42–43.

Chapter 10. Principle 7: Contribution

1 https://utmost.org/pouring-out-the-water-of-satisfaction/.

2 A. E. Goodenough, N. Little, W. S. Carpenter, and A. G. Hart, "Birds of a Feather Flock Together: Insights into Starling Murmuration Behaviour Revealed Using Citizen Science," *PLoS ONE* 12, No. 6 (2017): 2; e0179277. https://doi.org/10.1371/journal. Pone.0179277.

3 Ibid., 3.

4 Oswald Chambers, *My Utmost for His Highest.* https://utmost.org /pouring-out-the-water-of-satisfaction/.

5 Dabbawalas: http://mumbaidabbawala.in/.

6 Mehrdad Baghai and James Quigley, *As One: Individual Action, Collective Power* (New York: Portfolio/Penguin, 2011), 242.

7 Brenda Salter McNeil, *Roadmap to Reconciliation: Moving Communities into Unity, Wholeness, and Justice* (Downers Grove, IL: Intervarsity Press, 2015), 38.

8 Keith Ferazzi, *Never Eat Alone* (Expanded, updated edition. Currency, 2014).

Chapter 11. Radical Optimism

1 The phrase "radical optimism" was inspired from John Armstrong. See John Armstrong, *Your Church Is Too Small* (Grand Rapids, MI: Zondervan, 2014), 24.

2 Jim Collins coined the phrase a "big hairy audacious goal" or BHAG. See Jim Collins, *Built to Last* (New York: HarperCollins, 1994).

3 Peter M. Senge, *The Fifth Discipline: The Art and Practice of the Learning Organization* (New York: Doubleday Currency, 1990), 135.

4 On wild fires: http://www.nps.gov/fire/wildland-fire/learning-center/fire-in-depth/fireline-construction.cfm.

5 John Kotter, *Leading Change* (Cambridge, MA: Harvard Business Review Press, 1996).

6 Phil Knight, *Shoe Dog: A Memoir by the Creator of NIKE* (New York: Scribner's, 2016).

Chapter 12. Creating the MO

1 Francis Frangipane, *When the Many Are One: How to Lay Aside our Differences and Come Together as the House of God* (Lake Mary, FL: Charisma House, 2009), xv.

2 Paul Fleischmann, *Better Together: Discovering the Dynamic Results of Cooperation* (Oviedo, FL: HigherLife, 2015).

3 Phillip Butler, *Well Connected: Releasing Power and Restoring Hope Through Kingdom Partnerships* (Colorado Springs, CO: Authentic Publishing, 2006), 33.

4 Geoffrey Wainwright et al., *Ecumenical Theology in Worship, Doctrine, and Life: Essays Presented to Geoffrey Wainwright on His Sixtieth Birthday* (New York: Oxford University Press, 1999).

5 Malcolm Gladwell, *The Tipping Point: How Little Things Can Make a Big Difference* (Boston: Little, Brown, 2000), 12.

Chapter 13. Rules to Live By

1 Mehrdad Baghai and James Quigley, *As One: Individual Action Collective Power* (New York: Portfolio / Penguin, 2011).

2 Paul Fleischmann, *Better Together: Discovering the Dynamic Results of Cooperation* (Oviedo, FL: HigherLife, 2015), 105.

3 Homothymadon: https://www.blueletterbible.org/lang/lexicon/lexicon.cfm?t=kjv&strongs=g3661.

4 John Piper quote: http://www.desiringgod.org/articles/what-god-can-do-in-five-seconds.

5 Malcolm Gladwell, *The Tipping Point: How Little Things Can Make a Big Difference* (Boston: Little, Brown, 2000), 14, 32.

6 http://www.gordonconwell.edu/resources/Center-for-the-Study-of-Global-Christianity.cfm.

7 Bjørn Andersen and Tom Fagerhaug, *Root Cause Analysis: Simplified Tools and Techniques*, 2nd edition (Milwaukee, WI: ASQ Quality Press, 2006), 131. ProQuest ebrary. Web. August 25, 2015.

8 Brenda Salter McNeil, *Roadmap to Reconciliation: Moving Communities into Unity, Wholeness, and Justice* (Downers Grove, IL: Intervarsity Press, 2015), 33.

9 Phillip Butler, *Well Connected: Releasing Power and Restoring Hope Through Kingdom Partnerships* (Colorado Springs, CO: Authentic Publishing, 2006), 16, 50.

10 Andrea Cavagna, Alessio Cimarelli, Irene Giardina, Giorgio Parisi, Raffaele Santagati, Fabio Stefanini, et al., "Scale-Free Correlations in Starling Flocks," *PNAS Proceedings of the National Academy of Sciences* 107.26 (2010): 11865–11870. PsycINFO.

11 Jay W. Forrester, "The Beginning of System Dynamics," *McKinsey Quarterly* 4 (1995): 4–16. *Business Source Premier*. Web. August 25, 2015.

12 Thomas Merton, *No Man Is an Island* (Boston: Mariner Books, 2002), 120.

13 Peter M. Senge, *The Fifth Discipline: The Art and Practice of the Learning Organization* (New York: Doubleday Currency, 1990), 60.

14 Senge, *The Fifth Discipline*, 40.

15 Reinhold Niebuhr, *Moral Man and Immoral Society: A Study in Ethics and Politics* (New York & London: C. Scribner's, 1932).

16 Churchill quote: http://www.parliament.uk/about/living-heritage/ building/palace/architecture/palacestructure/churchill/.

17 Christena Cleveland, *Disunity in Christ: Uncovering the Hidden Forces That Keep Us Apart* (Downers Grove, IL: Intervarsity Press, 2013), 73.

Chapter 14: Let's GO!

1 Paul Fleischmann, *Better Together: Discovering the Dynamic Results of Cooperation* (Oviedo, FL: HigherLife, 2015), 54.

About the Authors

LUCAS RAMIREZ is a man remade by the great love of Christ. His journey started in Argentina, and at the age of six, he emigrated to the United States with his family. Now, Lucas lives out his passion for raising up the next generation of leaders in his role as CEO of The Gathering Place, an innovative student mentoring and Christian leadership development organization that impacts over ten thousand students annually. He is a keynote speaker and has spoken at venues such as Catalyst Conference, TEDx, and the Georgia House of Representatives. He is an organizational leadership expert and loves sharing and learning new ideas. The greatest blessing in his life is being married to his college sweetheart, Thea, and together they have three kids. Lucas thinks he might just be the luckiest guy alive. Read more at LucasRamirez.org and follow him @thelucasramirez.

MIKE DEVITO is a ministry veteran with over forty years of full-time ministry experience, both in the Pacific Northwest and Southern California. Mike frequently speaks at camps, conferences, and youth events. Because of his expertise in networking ministries, Mike is also a sought-after advisor and consultant to groups and pastor networks. Mike currently serves as the Southwest regional coordinator for the National Network of Youth Ministries, overseeing networks in five states. He also serves as the ministry outreach coordinator at Biola University in California. Mike lives in Orange County, California, with wife, Kristi, of forty-one years! They have two daughters and three grandchildren.